THE POWER OF receiving

Jeremy P. Tarcher/Penguin
A MEMBER OF PENGUIN GROUP (USA) INC.
New York

THE POWER OF

receiving

*A Revolutionary Approach to Giving Yourself
the Life You Want and Deserve*

AMANDA OWEN

JEREMY P. TARCHER/PENGUIN
Published by the Penguin Group
Penguin Group (USA) Inc., 375 Hudson Street, New York, New York 10014, USA •
Penguin Group (Canada), 90 Eglinton Avenue East, Suite 700, Toronto,
Ontario M4P 2Y3, Canada (a division of Pearson Penguin Canada Inc.) • Penguin Books Ltd,
80 Strand, London WC2R 0RL, England • Penguin Ireland, 25 St Stephen's Green,
Dublin 2, Ireland (a division of Penguin Books Ltd) • Penguin Group (Australia),
250 Camberwell Road, Camberwell, Victoria 3124, Australia (a division of
Pearson Australia Group Pty Ltd) • Penguin Books India Pvt Ltd, 11 Community Centre,
Panchsheel Park, New Delhi–110 017, India • Penguin Group (NZ), 67 Apollo Drive,
Rosedale, North Shore 0632, New Zealand (a division of Pearson New Zealand Ltd) •
Penguin Books (South Africa) (Pty) Ltd, 24 Sturdee Avenue, Rosebank, Johannesburg 2196,
South Africa

Penguin Books Ltd, Registered Offices: 80 Strand, London WC2R 0RL, England

Most Tarcher/Penguin books are available at special quantity discounts for bulk purchase for
sales promotions, premiums, fund-raising, and educational needs. Special books or book ex-
cerpts also can be created to fit specific needs. For details, write Penguin Group (USA) Inc.
Special Markets, 375 Hudson Street, New York, NY 10014.

Library of Congress Cataloging-in-Publication Data

Owen, Amanda.
    The power of receiving: a revolutionary approach to giving yourself the life you want and
deserve / Amanda Owen.
        p.   cm.
    ISBN 978-1-58542-817-5
    1. Need (Psychology).   2. Generosity.   3. Sharing.   4. Beneficiaries—Psychology.
I. Title.
    BF503.O94   2010   2010027765
    158—dc22

Printed in the United States of America
10 9 8 7 6 5 4 3

Book design by Jennifer Ann Daddio

I dedicate this book to all who give and give and give—including, but by no means limited to, mothers, fathers, grandparents, teachers, aid workers, health workers, case managers, social workers, nurses, doctors, psychologists, volunteers and caregivers.

I hope the information in this book will inspire you to receive.

THE WORLD WILL GIVE ONLY AS MUCH

AS YOU CAN RECEIVE

contents

CHAPTER TWO

introducing yourself to your goal:
creating the foundation
for your receive practice

CHAPTER THREE

helping your goal:
cultivating receiving

CHAPTER FOUR

deepening your relationship with your goal: *strengthening your capacity to receive*   107

CHAPTER FIVE

investing in your goal: *exercising your receive muscles*   126

CHAPTER EIGHT
strengthening your relationship with all of your goals: *your ongoing receive practice*

preface

A displaced Hurricane Katrina victim who had lost everything was on TV being interviewed in the living room of her relative's home in Ohio. I watched her bottom lip quiver as she tried to stop the tears that were running in rivulets down the crevices of her weary face.

She was upset—but not for the reason you would think. Her despair was due to having to receive help. A proud woman who had worked two jobs for most of her adult life, she had never "taken handouts" from anybody, and her shame was apparent by her inability to look at the interviewer, by her downcast eyes.

Twice traumatized, I noted—first from the flood and then from needing to receive. I was not surprised by her anguish, since by 2005, the year of the devastating Hurricane Katrina, I had been presenting lectures about the importance of receiving for more than a decade.

The sad truth is we are not taught how to receive, let alone educated to balance giving and receiving. This deficit causes so much suffering, so much trouble. While the Giver archetype is well-known and celebrated in our culture, its opposite, the Receiver, is almost wholly unfamiliar. The result? Busyness is a virtue, and countless people multitask themselves into exhaustion, overextend their energy reserves and take care of other people's needs at the expense of their own health and emotional well-being.

This investment in one side of the give/receive or active/receptive equation goes against nature. And a caregiving, überactive individual who forms an identity based upon this unnatural state pays a high price.

The woman on TV was used to giving help but not receiving it. And now without the identity raft that had kept her afloat throughout her life, she was in deeply unfamiliar territory, physically and emotionally.

Her story is not unusual although most of us are not

run out of town by a flood. More familiar scenarios are an empty nest, a loved one's death, a lost job, the onset of a health crisis or aging that brings a loss of independence and mobility.

At one time or another, we have been or will be in this Katrina victim's position—needing to turn to others for help, whether from relatives, friends, strangers or the government.

I doubt that receiving is a subject you have spent much time thinking about. Before my book begins, I want to tell you about how I stumbled upon this topic and how it changed my life and the lives of those I have taught how to receive.

I sold my house in 2007, left a dead-end relationship and drove west across the United States to start a new life in Arizona. I owe this radical change to my decision in 2004 to lead a group of eight people in a five-week Receive and Manifest course I created.

During the previous year I had written a manuscript titled *52 Reflections on the Art of Receiving,* which was based on almost two decades of research. This book provided tips and strategies—one for each week of the year—to help people create happier, healthier lives by bringing receiving into balance with giving.

Back in the mid-1980s I became interested in the subject of receiving through my counseling work. Many of my clients habitually overextended their giving, sacrificing their needs and desires to help others attain their goals. Attempts to get their mates, children, other family members, coworkers or friends to help them or be more giving were frequently ignored. Frustrated, weary and resentful, my clients asked, "When is it my turn?"

If you have ever tried to control other people's behavior, you know how futile that can be! Trying to force people to give is simply ineffective. As I sought ways to help my clients, I wondered if too much time and energy were focused on the un-giving instead of examining one's own capacity to receive. The more I thought about receiving, the more questions I had. What is receiving? How can I learn to receive? What are the benefits of knowing how to receive?

It didn't take me long to realize that because our culture lacks a vocabulary for receiving, to help my clients I would need to create one. I zeroed in on words that expressed receptivity of one sort or another. I studied Buddhist teachings, the philosophy of the Tao and the physics of quantum theory. I studied how people chased away what other people tried to give to them. I looked for the cultural underpinnings that supported a life philosophy that puts a halo around giving and ignores receiving. I examined the ways that people exclude their own needs and investigated the reasons that led them to do so.

From this research, I knew I would need to find a way for people to view the act of receiving as valuable, natural and advantageous to their happiness. And I needed to create concrete, easy exercises that people could—and would—integrate into their busy lives.

Eventually I developed the Three Steps to Receiving and began to teach my clients the foundational tools they needed to learn how to receive. Their lives changed for the better as they developed healthier give-and-take (or receive) relationships. My life also began to shift as my knowledge of and experience with receiving deepened.

Based on what I was witnessing, I knew others could benefit from what I had learned. In 2003, I submitted my manuscript *52 Reflections on the Art of Receiving* to agents and publishers. Those who got back to me had reservations.

"Why would people feel the need to receive?" they asked. "It is a topic that few have ever thought about. Where would the book be shelved—under what category?"

People were not receptive to a book about receiving! I realized I needed to express my ideas more clearly. Back to square one.

People's awareness of topics related to receiving has grown significantly since 2003. The movie *The Secret*, literature that features the Law of Attraction, and the ongoing plea from Oprah and others for overdoing, exhausted people to give to themselves—these have all given me a receptive world that is more educated and open to learning about the benefits of receiving.

But back in 2003, I didn't have the benefit of this educated public. As I mulled over my ideas about receiving and reviewed my manuscript, it occurred to me that in addition to helping people live more balanced lives, knowing how to receive might also help them get what they want—it could facilitate manifestation. If my hunch was correct, I could include information about this connection in a rewritten manuscript.

My hypothesis was this: life is inherently giving and if barriers to receiving were removed, like when a floodgate is lowered, life's givingness would rush in. By this time, I was familiar with the benefits of receiving when it came to creating reciprocity in relationships and a greater balance in one's life overall. But the idea that someone could actually manifest a goal if they were an experienced Receiver intrigued me. And it seemed logical.

Doesn't it make sense that if you want something—whether to meet the love of your life, get a great job or increase your financial stability—you need to know how to receive it? After all, how can the world give to you if you can't or don't know how to receive? Even those well versed in the Law of Attraction have discovered that just because you know how to attract something doesn't mean you know how to receive it. Receiving something as simple as a compliment is difficult for many people.

I put out the word to my clients: meet with me for two hours, once a week, for five weeks, to manifest a goal. Eight people signed up for the experiment.

What occurred in that five-week course astounded us. Not only did many of our goals manifest but also something deep and profound shifted in how we looked at life. We *saw* the world differently. And this happened after only five weeks! I was clearly onto something. I felt that I had discovered the right key for the right lock. That key? Receptivity—the ability to receive.

As word spread about the extraordinary results that had occurred, that first class led to many others. Instead of completing my book, I spent the next four years teaching people how to cultivate and strengthen their capacity to receive, while I continually tweaked my Receive and Manifest course and deepened my understanding of the relationship between receptivity and manifestation. And through the process of helping others manifest their dreams, I began to manifest many of my own.

Ultimately I set that first manuscript aside as I focused on the nuts-and-bolts mechanism of manifestation. I wanted people to know that receiving not only creates balanced lives and relationships but it also has the power to lead us to our hopes, goals and dreams. The book you hold in your hands is the result of these last six years—the book I began writing in Pennsylvania and finished in Arizona.

In *The Power of Receiving*, I show you how to restore balance to your life and manifest your hopes, dreams and goals. I include easy, simple power-of-receiving exercises that you can do anytime, anywhere and achieve life-changing results.

The interrelationship between activity and receptivity has been written about by many wise poets and philosophers over the eons. My goal is to teach these universal principles in modern-day terms that are supported by practices you can immediately apply to your life. In this spirit, I offer you here the wise words of Lao-tzu and a contemporary translation:

*The created universe carries the yin at its back
and the yang in front;
Through the union of the pervading principles it
reaches harmony.*

—LAO-TZU

Twenty-first-Century Translation:

*As far as boyfriends go, Paulie Bleeker is totally boss.
He is the cheese to my macaroni.*

—JUNO MACGUFF from the movie *Juno*

a final note

If you are like me, you have read plenty of self-help books in which you skimmed right past the exercises that are designed to help you achieve whatever the book is offering. Please don't skip the exercises in *The Power of Receiving*. Take your time and do each one in order and for the time prescribed. As you deepen your knowledge of and experience with the world of receiving, you will enjoy spectacular concrete results. But they are predicated on doing the exercises, most of which require less than two minutes. This small amount of time will produce an extraordinary shift in your consciousness and in your life.

To support you, a Resource Guide at the back of this book has additional information to support your Receive Practice. Or go to my website, www.ThePowerofReceiving .com.

—Amanda

introduction

Just outside of Philadelphia, buddleia plants appear each summer. They are more commonly known as butterfly bushes—a name earned because butterflies are drawn like a magnet to their bright colors and sweet fragrance. These delicate creatures drink the nectar, and as they move from flower to flower, they carry sticky pollen from one butterfly bush to another.

The survival of these lovely plants is dependent upon being able to attract their pollinators—the butterflies that drink the nectar that ensures, in turn, their own continued existence.

Nature provides many such examples of mutual interdependence, of giving and receiving. Yet even though we are participants in nature's cooperative interplay, it is easy to make the mistake of thinking that something happens because we alone make it happen. When we view our actions as the only measuring stick, we look at what we do within an isolated and unnatural context. This encourages us to exaggerate the importance of initiative and to allocate most, if not all, of our resources toward the active pursuit of our goals.

Achieving a goal by attracting it—inviting it to move toward us—just like the butterfly is drawn to the butterfly bush, is an idea that has only recently entered mainstream thinking. Many people who have heard of and are excited about the Law of Attraction are inexperienced with the vocabulary of receiving and are therefore unsure of how to implement these important ideas.

The more aware we are of the interdependent nature of our lives, the clearer becomes our view of ourselves, our environment and our goals. Who is the Giver and who is the Receiver when we look at the relationship between a butterfly and a butterfly bush? They give to each other and receive from each other; both are fulfilling their goals.

If butterfly bushes were to approach their goal the way we have been taught, this is what it might look like:

Each summer butterfly bushes would run around the neighborhood, waving their blossoms trying to convince butterflies that they are the best butterfly bush around and that the butterflies should follow *them* home and pollinate *their* flowers.

If we were to view this from a perspective of male and female roles, then the stereotypical female version might look something like this:

To compete with other butterfly bushes, great attention would be paid to the flowers and their shapes. Some would get fake blossoms. Others would decorate their leaves and stems.

The efforts directed toward beauty enhancement and developing tantalizing fragrances would consume so much time and attention that some of the bushes would become ill due to being out of their fertile soil.

The psychological toll of competition, of leaving their home ground and of watching other plants get more butterflies would leave its mark in low self-esteem and diminished confidence.

The stereotypical male version might look something like this:

The butterfly bushes would show off their capacity to "deliver the goods" by boasting of their track record, their superior fragrance and the number of butterflies they attracted in the past. Fatigue would eventually settle in when the energy it takes to cavort around the neighborhood undermines their capacity to showcase their best blossoms. The energy required to keep up with younger, faster bushes would lead to diminished health and vitality. But they would not want anyone to know that they are not feeling well, as this might lead butterflies to search elsewhere for more virile, nectar-producing plants.

The psychological toll of competition and time away from their home ground would eventually result in diminished confidence and low self-esteem.

Isn't it amusing to contemplate objects of nature behaving this way? Doesn't it seem silly and like a waste of time and energy? Yet how often have you chased a goal, perhaps a job or a relationship, and ended up feeling as depleted as these butterfly bushes?

Our culture has long operated from a paradigm that champions the use of willpower and under-recognizes the value of receptivity. Expecting to achieve a goal by utilizing only our will and determination is a recipe for burnout. Essentially that is what we are doing when all our efforts are geared toward the active pursuit of our goals.

In contrast, creating a plan that includes strategies for attracting as well as pursuing allows us to recognize and receive what the world and people have to offer us. And when giving and receiving are equal partners, you simply have a better chance of manifesting your goals.

While a lack of reciprocity in a relationship and being unable to manifest a dream may seem like two separate problems, they are in fact rooted in the same infertile soil. Those who do not know how to receive are attracted to those who do not give. Those same people invariably refuse the very help that would enable them to manifest their dreams.

who should read this book?

WOMEN
(MORE FOR YOU MEN BELOW)

I have a goal. I want every woman who appears before TV's Judge Judy, trying to get back the money she loaned to her ex-boyfriend, ex-spouse, ex-friend or family member, to be given a copy of *The Power of Receiving* as she leaves the courtroom. I'm almost there!

When I tell people what my book is about, I invariably

hear, "My [mom/friend/coworker/daughter] needs to read your book! She doesn't know how to receive at all! She won't even receive a compliment!" Notice that I use the word "she."

I wrote *The Power of Receiving* for men as well as women. I discuss in my book the specific roles that women and men play in our culture, and how receiving will benefit both. However, women, whether as an innate characteristic or as a consequence of their socialization, pay attention to and tend to others' needs in a way that makes them vulnerable to overextending their giving and subjugating their own needs and desires.

Whether you are a single mom trying to balance work with care for your children and a social life or you are looking after an elderly parent, the reality is that these roles fall largely to women. Although many men play out these roles, their numbers pale by comparison to the number of women who find themselves in these situations. Nurses, counselors, social workers and others in the helping fields? Ditto. They're mostly women.

Ask a woman to be selfish and to think of her own needs and you will not get anywhere. Women are reluctant to embrace philosophies that ask them to promote their needs over others'. They are not looking to "trade places." But women easily welcome the concept of inclusion and the importance of reciprocity. Relational by nature, they "get" that bringing their relationships and their lives into balance can be accomplished by putting the *receive* into *give and receive*. And they are excited about what learning to receive has to offer.

The Power of Receiving promotes a philosophy that values receiving as much as giving and is for any woman who does too much, loves too much or multitasks herself into exhaustion.

MEN

It's a well-worn joke that men refuse to ask for directions or consult a map. More seriously, in regard to your health, many of you would sooner die than ask for help—and some do. Many women report that getting their husbands or partners to go to the doctor is next to impossible. It's no wonder! Men: you have been raised to be strong, self-reliant and to never show your feelings. What does this have to do with receiving? Doesn't it make sense that if you want to receive something, it helps to know how to ask for it?

Even though countless women have difficulty receiving from others, people in general are still more comfortable with a woman saying she needs help or to receive something than they are when a man makes the same request. This is easy to see in an extreme of homelessness. Do you react differently when you see a woman or a man living on the streets?

Yet, just like women, you want relationships that add to instead of detract from your life. You want to be appreciated for all that you do. For that to occur, your receiving skills need to be strong.

The Power of Receiving shows you how to create a life where everything that you do is returned tenfold by grateful mates, appreciative children, thankful bosses and hardworking employees and coworkers.

CAREGIVERS

There is little doubt that helping others brings many benefits to the giver—and such generosity is to be encouraged. But when we give to others while ignoring our own needs, we can experience unintended consequences including physical exhaustion, resentment and feelings of failure. This is especially true if you are a caregiver.

How do you take care of and give to yourself when so much of your time is devoted to caring for others? If you are a caregiver, you need help!

Yet there are remarkably few avenues of assistance or

books that offer insights and strategies to help you negotiate this emotional territory. Although support groups are plentiful, especially online, many people never avail themselves of this assistance. And while traditional and alternative practitioners urge people to take care of themselves, all of the messages or services in the world from gym membership credits to healthy diet instructions to spa treatments do no good if you don't use them.

For caregivers of elderly parents, ill family members and friends, *The Power of Receiving* gives you a twenty-first-century solution that shows you how to include *you* in your goals to help and heal those you love.

THE HELPING PROFESSIONS

Compassion fatigue is a frequently used term in the helping professions. Many who are drawn to this work suffer from an inability to turn off the "giving" instinct in their personal relationships. These include nurses, social workers and therapists and even those who volunteer.

If you devote your working life to helping others, you already know the consequences of not taking care of yourself. Whether you are vulnerable to health ailments because of overwork and exhaustion, have an unsatisfactory or nonexistent social life because you are too tired to go anywhere, or regularly exceed your energy limits to give time and attention to your family—you need help!

Receiving is a skill that can be learned, developed and strengthened. *The Power of Receiving* gives you a nut-and-bolts plan that will help you bring more balance into your life and greater reciprocity in your relationships. In turn, you will become healthier and more energized and your giving will no longer drain you—it will strengthen you.

NEW AGE, METAPHYSICAL, SPIRITUAL AND SELF-HELP READERS

As people look for relief in an increasingly fast-paced world, many are turning to alternative ideas for insight. If you count yourself as a member of this group, you are interested in philosophies that teach you how to manifest your desires by changing the way you think.

Perhaps you've read Eckhart Tolle's *A New Earth* or seen the movie *The Secret* based on the book by Rhonda Byrnes. You may meditate, recite positive affirmations or keep a gratitude journal. You understand the concept of Unity consciousness and try to live your life in a spirit of compassion for others while developing goals for yourself.

If you would like to further your education or if you have been stymied by a lack of progress in attaining your goals, the ideas in this book will help you.

The Power of Receiving will give you new tools, deepen your understanding of manifestation and add to your repertoire. It will teach you how to receive what you are attracting.

how this book is organized

Chapter 1, "Attracting Your Goal: Understanding Receiving," provides a basic education in the art of receiving. The definition and value of receiving are discussed to give you a working Receive vocabulary. Here you will learn how to develop the Receive Muscles necessary to attract a goal, just as a butterfly bush attracts butterflies.

Chapter 2, "Introducing Yourself to Your Goal: Creating the Foundation for Your Receive Practice," shows you how to create a goal and presents the basic three steps that provide the foundation for a successful Receive practice.

Chapter 3, "Helping Your Goal: Cultivating Receiving," explores and redefines basic cultural misconceptions that can prevent goals from manifesting.

Chapter 4, "Deepening Your Relationship with Your

Goal: Strengthening Your Capacity to Receive," introduces the Big Circle and Little Circle to help you conceptualize the mechanics of manifestation.

Chapter 5, "Investing in Your Goal: Exercising Your Receive Muscles," offers tools and exercises to help create a lasting, successful relationship with your goal.

Chapter 6, "What Stands Between You and Your Goal? Embracing Receiving," presents the Monster Celebration, an exercise to help you integrate what hasn't been received and welcomed into your life.

Chapter 7, "Love Your Goal and It Will Love You Back: Bringing Receiving and Giving into Balance," provides examples of people who, by strengthening their receptivity, have successfully manifested their goals in the areas of relationships, career, money, health and weight loss.

Chapter 8, "Strengthening Your Relationship with All of Your Goals: Your Ongoing Receive Practice," reviews the Power of Receiving philosophy and provides a summary of the Power of Receiving exercises. Here you will find resources for additional support and inspiration to support your Receive Practice.

And now, turn the page and get ready to receive!

CHAPTER ONE

attracting your goal

Understanding Receiving

are you a receiver?

Definition of receive: *"to accept willingly."*

Imagine this: You are relaxing at home while your spouse makes dinner and your children tend to their chores. As you read your favorite magazine, you sigh with contentment. Life is good.

You probably already know that reducing stress is a good thing. Yet, in a world that has elevated busyness to a virtue and has convinced you that doing for others is more important than giving to yourself, how do you create a life where what you give is in balance with what you receive? How do you set aside guilt-free time for *you*?

Take a look at the following. Do any of these scenarios describe your life?

- You are the one people turn to when they need help. If you didn't screen your phone calls and leave e-mail unanswered, you'd never get any downtime at all.
- You spend so much time working that the important people in your life complain they never get to spend time with you.
- You enjoyed your recent vacation, but it took you a couple of days to remember how to relax and now you dread going back to work.
- Your parents are living with you, and the stresses of their care are leaving you feeling overwhelmed.
- You have a job where you help others (nurse, social worker, teacher, secretary, etc.). When you are worn out and in need of a little TLC, family members and friends are unavailable.
- You are a single parent and don't know where

you would find the time or energy for anything that is not devoted to making a living and raising your children.

Do any of the above examples sound familiar? If not, congratulate yourself because it is likely that your giving and receiving are in balance, meaning that sometimes you are the Giver and other times the Receiver. If this is you, your natural state is feeling physically rested, mentally alert and engaged, emotionally content and spiritually fulfilled.

If you can't recall when you last felt rested, alert, content and fulfilled—keep reading.

Symptoms of a non-Receiver

Let's begin with the following statements. Do you identify with any of them?

- Emotionally you feel unappreciated.
- Physically you feel exhausted.
- Mentally you feel resentful.
- Spiritually you feel depleted.

Statements of a non-Receiver

Are these familiar?

- People take advantage of me.
- I don't get what I want.
- I feel taken for granted.
- I'm always there for others; no one is there for me.
- People don't listen to me.
- I can't count on anyone.
- The only way something gets done is if I do it.
- I know what is good for other people but I don't know what I want.

Although it can be tempting to blame other people for your circumstances, if you have not cultivated reciprocity in your relationships, I invite you to entertain the following statement.

The only possible match for someone who doesn't know how to receive is someone who doesn't know how to give.

Non-Receivers are drawn to non-Givers. In other words, the problem is not that you have been drawn to non-giving people, but that you are an inexperienced Receiver. The reason this is an important distinction is that you can't control others' behavior; you can only control your own.

You can learn to become a Receiver. I am going to show you how.

do you know how to receive?

Definition of receptive: *"ready or willing to receive."*

I imagine you are familiar with the maxim *it is better to give than to receive*. You have probably been taught about the importance of giving. Giving to others can feel rewarding. Receiving can also. We are grateful when our partners are generous, our children considerate and our bosses appreciative.

Yet how often have you turned away what people offer you, whether it's a compliment, picking up the check at lunch or even an apology? How many times have you wanted life to give to you but found yourself saying, "Oh, don't worry about me . . . I'm fine." It's the equivalent of the old martyr joke: "That's all right. I'll just sit here in the dark."

What happens when you don't have experience in receiving? You are likely to believe the following statements:

- Wanting something for yourself is unseemly at best and greedy and selfish at worst.
- You shouldn't burden others with your troubles.
- People who achieve success without help are admirable.
- Those who achieve success while enduring significant hardship are even more admirable.

You are also likely to feel uncomfortable asking for what you want unless the following conditions are met:

- It doesn't make others uncomfortable, upset, or angry.
- It doesn't interfere with what people want for themselves.
- It doesn't interfere with what someone wants for you.
- People agree with you.

However, when *you* are the one who wants to give, it's easy to see how silly it is for someone to refuse what you offer, whether that is assistance of some kind or a gift. It's frustrating! Interestingly, a person who rebuffs your help is often the same individual who frequently complains, "I feel taken for granted and unappreciated; no one takes my needs into account."

The following story illustrates this paradox.

A man and his family are trapped in their house with rising floodwaters closing in fast.

"Please help us," the man prays to God.

After a while, someone comes by in a rowboat and says, "Climb in!"

"That's all right," the man replies, "Go help someone else. I'm praying to God, who will save us." He continues to pray. The waters rise and the family is forced to crawl up on top of the roof. The man continues to pray.

A helicopter flies overhead and rope is dropped.

"That's okay. Go help someone else. I am praying to God, who will save us." The helicopter moves on and the man continues to pray . . . all the way up to the time that the waters rise and the family is drowned.

Shocked, the man later complains to God, "I have served you faithfully. Why didn't you answer my prayers?"

"I did," God replies. "I sent you a boat and a helicopter."

We want life to give to us, but we turn the gift away when it shows up!

why receive?

Definition of reciprocity: *"a mode of exchange in which transactions take place between individuals who are symmetrically placed—i.e., they are exchanging as equals, neither being in a dominant position."*

Although increasing receptivity helps you achieve your goals, the idea seems counterintuitive because it really doesn't feel like you are *doing* anything to advance your cause. Yet being a good observer (a receptive state) enhances the ability to analyze (an active state), and relaxation (a receptive state) is advantageous to thinking (an active state).

Receptive States

Meditating	Listening	Feeling grateful	Accepting
Allowing	Opening	Relaxing	Letting go
Noticing	Observing	Welcoming	Yielding
Including	Embracing	Feeling	Hearing
Appreciating	Being	Contemplating	Watching
Letting be	Attracting	Revealing	Acknowledging

Active States

Analyzing	Talking	Investigating	Controlling
Influencing	Promoting	Multitasking	Persuading
Defining	Judging	Exploring	Shaping
Pushing	Holding	Thinking	Informing
Building	Doing	Acting	Performing
Going after	Hiding	Forcing	Evaluating

A skilled Receiver is one who excels in the ability to experience each of the receptive states listed above. If you are *multitasking* much of the time (from the Active States list), you may not know how to *allow* (from the Receptive States list) events to unfold when appropriate; you may not even *notice* (from the Receptive list) something that could be helpful to you. Or if you are extremely *talkative* (from the Active States list), you are less likely to excel at *listening* (from the Receptive States list).

When you rely almost exclusively on activity, your will is overtaxed. There is no replenishment time. It's easy to see this in the person who is constantly on the go. Eventually the body, emotions or the mind tend to rebel. The body may become sick, the emotions frazzled or the mind scattered. It's like trying to keep a bunch of balls in the air all the time. It's exhausting.

Valuing what receiving has to offer (the experiences in the Receptive States list) helps you attract what you want. When you practice receiving, you give the will (the experiences in the Active States list) a chance to rest and to feel supported.

Think of your life. Do you see that when one person does all of the "doing," the other stands back? If you are the one who is always busy, chances are you'll feel exhausted and even resentful. We like it when we are in balance with others. Think of the active and receptive as a team in which all members are pulling their own weight.

the difference between a taker and a receiver

For every Giver there is a Receiver. For every Doer there is a Taker.

Namaste: I honor the God in you that is in me is a Sanskrit greeting and blessing that beautifully illustrates the unity of life. Just like this greeting, both genuine giving and genuine receiving are acts of recognition of the other, acknowledgments of our sameness, of our humanity. When we give or receive generosity, we vibrate to the same chord—we are a melody of One. Together, giving and receiving form a connection. Energy moves out in giving and returns in receiving.

Do you think of the word *giving* as something one does? Many of us make little if any distinction between something that is done because we *want* to do it and something that is done because we believe we *have* to do it. Even so, how you feel after doing something for someone who has an attitude of ingratitude is likely to be markedly different from how you feel after giving to someone who is sincerely grateful. Reciprocity is inbuilt when the Receiver acknowledges the giving. It is one of the ways a Receiver gives back to the Giver.

It is a one-sided equation with Doers and Takers. The Doer does not receive anything back from the Taker. The energy goes out in doing—and goes out and goes out and goes out—with nothing or little coming back. If you have experienced this kind of relationship, then you have probably felt drained by many of your interactions. You also may have felt upset about a basic lack of fairness.

Even when experiencing this inequality, many people continue to give, not because they feel a genuine desire to do so, but because of an internal expectation about how "one *should* behave." Nonetheless, we feel the dissonance with this kind of giving—a "doing" born out of an expectation that has little to do with our authentic feelings.

It is the same when someone takes instead of receives. Taking is not a receptive act. Takers pull and yank and tug. They sulk, pout and manipulate. They use and exploit. They feel entitled; they expect people to cater to them. Interestingly, when people take there is never enough, they are never filled up. They want more and more.

The person who *does* and the person who *takes* are not energized or emotionally fulfilled by their interactions. The person who *gives* and the one who *receives* experience their connection; it is a mutually fulfilling transaction. The first is an experience of separation, the second of unity. One stems from a feeling of lack and the other from wholeness.

To achieve a goal, letting go of old definitions of receiving and giving is essential. Because I am presenting a very different approach to giving and receiving, the next chapters explore this concept further and will answer many of the questions you may have at this point. For now, understanding that *doing* and *taking* cause separation, while *giving* and *receiving* create connection, will help you build a basic foundation for achieving your goals.

a receiver is not a doormat

Definition of receptivity: *"a willingness or readiness to receive impressions or ideas."*

"In my day, as a woman, you had to be tough or you weren't going to get anything or go anywhere. People will walk all over you if you're passive. I can't do it; being passive is against my nature!" This kind of declaration is how many people react when they are introduced to the concept that receiving is beneficial.

If you are unfamiliar with the vocabulary of receiving, it is easy to be confused about the difference between passivity and receptivity.

The dictionary definition of *passive* is "to be influenced or acted upon without exerting influence or acting in return." A synonym for *passive* is *submissive*. In contrast, receptivity is a dynamic and energized state. When we are receptive, we are actively engaged, open and interested as in these examples:

- When you say, "She was receptive to my plan about carpooling," you are not saying she was passive or that she didn't care about the plan.

- When you say, "He was receptive to my idea of helping out at the soup kitchen on Thanksgiving," you are not saying that he is uninterested in the idea.
- When you say, "My child is receptive his new teacher's style of teaching," you are not talking about passivity at all!

The following examples further illustrate the energetic component of receptivity:

- Successful poker players utilize the receptive state when they observe the other players and remain relaxed. This helps them know when to hold and when to fold their cards. If they played without receiving the cues and clues from their environment, they would miss information that would help them make beneficial decisions.
- An effective physician is one who receives by listening to the patient and by observing conditions in the body. This takes expertise and energy. Physicians who are intent on imparting information without taking into account the

patient's experience miss the feedback that could sharpen their diagnostic skills.

- An owner of a thriving business pays attention to and delivers what his or her customers want. Success is the result of the owner's receptivity. Those who make decisions without customer feedback miss an opportunity to strengthen their business.

If you want something, you need to initiate an activity. However, if you never pause to watch the results and to assess what you have set in motion, you will miss information that will help you.

The environment and the people in it inform you of your progress. If you are stymied by a lack of results from what you have initiated, *observe*, *listen* and *allow* (all words from the Receptive States word list) to help you see the course you need to set to obtain the best results.

As you can see, receptivity is not at all passive. It takes quite a bit of energy to interpret the environment and to be an effective witness of what has been set in motion.

When we are not adept Receivers, we try to control everything through our own efforts. Not only is this counterproductive but such a strategy also does not take anything else or anybody's desires into account.

Think of receptivity as an energized and dynamic state to help you make the distinction between passivity and receptivity.

enabling is not giving

Give a man a fish and he will eat for a day. Teach a man to fish and he will eat for a lifetime.

—CHINESE PROVERB

Have you ever helped someone as a favor, only to discover that he or she continues to expect the same assistance? While being needed can feel great, when you give indefinitely or at levels beyond your capacity or comfort zone, it signals a lack of balance between the active and receptive principles.

How do you know whether you are enabling rather than giving? Enabling behavior is when you habitually do something for people that they are perfectly able to do for themselves. You also are enabling when you do something that prevents people from experiencing the consequences of their actions. Here are a few examples:

- A mother who constantly picks up after her children rather than teaching them to put their things away

- A husband who buys his alcoholic wife alcohol
- A person who covers for her coworker's habitual tardiness by doing that person's work
- A parent who continually takes care of or financially supports her adult child
- Someone who constantly "loans" money to a gambling-addicted friend

Some people "help" to demonstrate the virtue of giving in the hope that the recipient will want to reciprocate. In reality, the more one does, the more the recipient takes—and often with little or no gratitude!

The following quotation from Dennis Wholey illustrates the skewed thinking that giving naturally engenders appreciation and consideration.

Expecting the world to treat you fairly because you are a good person is a little like expecting the bull not to attack you because you are a vegetarian.

How do you tell whether you are *doing* rather than *giving?* Frequent anger and resentment toward the person you are helping are emotional signals indicating that something is not right. Giving and receiving are interconnected and mutually energizing and replenishing. It feels good to give and you feel blessed to receive.

Giving and receiving cannot always occur in balance within a specific relationship because of particular circumstances, such as caring for a physically or mentally ill individual. If you are in a situation in which the person does not have the ability to reciprocate, seek out someone who *can* give to you.

Caregivers need to replenish themselves, and fortunately there are organizations to support those who are caring for elderly or ill family members and others who require care. Support systems are also available through online communities. However, it is up to *you* to help yourself by connecting with existing support systems. Not only will doing so help you retain your own balance between being active and receptive but the recipients of your giving will also benefit.

Keep the following in mind when thinking about the differences between giving and enabling:

- When we enable, we habitually put other people's needs ahead of and at the expense of our own.
- Doing *more* is not an effective strategy to get others to be giving.
- Increasing your capacity to receive gives you the energy and resources to give.

- Receiving is replenishing and energizing, which in turn is helpful to the people under your care.
- Skilled Receivers are attracted to not only those to whom they can give, but also to those who can give to them.

receive everything—decide later

Nature does not hurry, yet everything is accomplished.

—LAO-TZU

Mother Teresa, for example, or doctors from Doctors Without Borders are considered Givers. Perhaps your grandma, your son's teacher or your best friend is on that list also. When we say someone is a Giver, we are saying that person has a generous heart. It's not a sometimes thing. We identify this generosity as a core part of his or her personality.

Have you ever said, "That person is such a fabulous Receiver!"? As funny as that may be to contemplate, being a Receiver is just the same as a being a Giver. It's in the core of the person.

Although it may seem counterintuitive, skilled Receivers have healthier boundaries than those who do not know how to receive. Because they have more data to work with, they set their boundaries appropriately based on that information, on what they know.

Just as a Giver doesn't feel compelled to hand over everything that is requested, a Receiver doesn't feel obliged to do, think or say anything that doesn't feel comfortable. Being an excellent Receiver does not rob you of using your good judgment, just as being a Giver doesn't mean that you are unable to use common sense. In fact, your ability to discern and discriminate is enhanced by the ability to receive. Experienced Receivers have more to work with than non-Receivers because they aren't blocking any of the following:

- Information from and about other people
- Information from the environment
- Information about their feelings

Receive everything—decide later. This means you should receive all of the data from your environment, including the inner environment of your feelings. You can decide later about what you want to do with what you have received.

How many times have you wished you had paid more attention to something that in retrospect would have been beneficial to you? Opening up your receptors helps you to be better informed about what you do and do not want. Often, the only reason we don't fully understand circumstances, people or events is because we never really received them to begin with. Instead, we pay attention to what we *want* to hear instead of what is actually being said.

The more you receive, the more likely you will make appropriate choices. Conversely, people who don't receive are often "flying blind," making decisions without all of the relevant data. This is usually much easier to see in other people.

Here are a few examples of statements from non-Receivers:

- He promised that for sure this year he'd leave his wife right after Christmas.
- She's a good kid. She didn't mean to steal that money.
- I don't know why I'm gaining weight. I'm barely eating!
- His teacher just doesn't appreciate his spunky personality.
- He didn't mean to hit me.

What might the people of the above statements be ignoring or not receiving? What choices would they make if they allowed themselves to sit for a while with their circumstances and their feelings, rather than excusing, deflecting or being mystified?

When people continually make excuses for another's actions or are baffled by the consequences of their own or someone else's behavior, it indicates they have filters that are blocking information. Or, as Henry Miller once wrote, "Confusion is a word for an order not yet understood."

Why would anybody want to block information? Here are a few reasons:

- Not wanting to experience your feelings
- Not wanting to look like a bad person
- Not wanting to disappoint others
- Not wanting to let people know how you really feel
- Wanting to avoid conflict

Are you familiar with the language of your feelings? When someone asks you how you feel about something, do you have to think about it? Or do you know?

Not knowing what you feel, not wanting to disappoint people and avoiding conflict may be habits you have cultivated over time. It takes courage to be honest with yourself and others. And it can be painful to fully experience your feelings about an unrewarding job or the effects of a destructive relationship.

How would you feel if you received any of the following?

- Information about your poor health
- Unhappiness with your marriage
- Distress about your working environment
- Anger at your invalid mother
- Resentment toward your child

Use the statement *Receive everything—decide later* to remind yourself to pause, wait and give yourself time. These are some of the benefits you receive:

- You are giving yourself all available data.
- You increase your options.
- You give yourself time to explore your choices.
- You are more likely to be happy with your decisions.
- You are unlikely to be in denial.
- You are more apt to make realistic decisions based on where you are *now*, instead of where you wish you were.

The next section more fully explores how healthy boundaries are a feature of people who know how to receive.

if i accept the gift, do i owe the giver?

And what desert greater shall there be, than that which lies in the courage and the confidence, nay the charity, of receiving.

—Kahlil Gibran

"If I let them buy me lunch, take my child to the fair, give me a gift—what will I owe them?"

Have you ever felt that you will have to do something you don't want to just because you accepted a gift or help? The concern about creating an obligation is an issue for many people. Here is an example:

Linda's husband died after a lingering illness. Although she had limited coping skills for managing the logistics of her life, she frequently turned down invitations from parents of her children's friends for sleepovers. Having time alone would have been a welcome relief, but feeling unable to reciprocate, she declined these offers.

Would the parents understand her inability to give in return? Knowing her circumstances is probably why the invitations kept coming in the first place! And the truth is, had she been able to receive the gift of time to herself, Linda would have had more energy to give to her own children. There are times when it is not possible or even prudent to return a favor. The Random Acts of Kindness movement is all about just this—passing on a kindness to someone other than the one who performed a good deed for you.

Here are a few questions to consider when someone wants to do something for you:

- Are you concerned with what someone will think of you if you don't reciprocate?
- Are you concerned with what *you* will think of you if you don't reciprocate?
- Do you think most people have ulterior motives when they want to do something for you?
- Do you feel undeserving of anyone doing something for you?
- Are you afraid you will have to do something you don't want to do if you let someone do something for you?

An experienced Receiver does not fear being indebted to a Giver because the gate of giving and receiving swings both ways—receiving sometimes and giving at other times. It is only when you don't have practice at both that it is easy to be confused about what your needs and rights are.

Chapter 3 explores this issue further through the examination of how we think of ourselves as good or bad people. But first, in chapter 2, you will learn how to create and nurture a goal.

introducing yourself to your goal

*Creating the Foundation for
Your Receive Practice*

getting your goal's attention

Goals are dreams with a deadline.

—NAPOLEON HILL

Throughout this book, I refer to your goal as "someone" with whom you are in a relationship. This personification is used as a device to help you communicate clearly what you want, which in turn helps you attain your goal.

With that said, let's get you on your goal's radar screen. It needs to know that you exist! This will require that you communicate with your goal. So smile, say hello and let it know what you want.

You would think, since you have had plenty of goals throughout your life, that it would be simple to write one of them down. Yet many people have no idea about how to state a goal in a way that leads to its manifestation. Below I have tips that help you connect quickly with your goal.

seven tips for effective goal writing

WRITE DOWN ONLY ONE GOAL

The reason that I advise starting with only one goal is so that you can give it your undivided attention. Once you write it down, you have begun a relationship. You want your goal to know that you are not going to be distracted by requests from other goals. Otherwise it's kind of like dating more than one person—doable perhaps depending on your sensibilities, but not ideal. Would you want to be out to dinner with a date and have him or her talking on the phone or texting someone else?

The other reason I think it's a good idea to concentrate on one goal at a time is that it gives you experience in taking your goal from inception to completion. Many, many goals never get enough oomph to manifest simply because too little attention is paid to them. Can you blame a goal for feeling lukewarm about you or wanting to find someone else—someone who will relate to, tend to, focus on and appreciate it?

WRITE DOWN YOUR GOAL IN ONE SENTENCE

Writing your goal in one sentence forces you to be clear about what you want. People love it when you are concise. Nobody likes to play guessing games or to be held hostage listening to a long rambling list of requests or demands! It's the same with your goal. So make sure your sentence is specific and concise.

Do not agonize over this though. Just get started. You are at the beginning of a relationship, and like any relationship, it will change over time as your needs and your goal's desires become clearer.

When you write a complete sentence rather than just a phrase or word, you demonstrate a full commitment. Plus, it's respectful and thoughtful. For instance, if you want to lose weight, you could write down your goal like this: *lose four pounds*. But it's as if you were to approach a personal trainer and say, "Lose four pounds." It comes across like you are too lazy to even say a full sentence!

Instead write: "My goal is to lose four pounds by the

end of two weeks." It's a strong statement. It's a declaration. Not only would a trainer know exactly what you want and be eager to work with you, but so will your goal!

The following are two examples from students who attended my five-week Receive and Manifest course. The first is an example of too much information and the second is just right.

First student's goal:

I am manifesting $280,500 to pay off private debts by the end of July. During class I will have completed the steps necessary and put together all marketing required for this manifestation to occur through real estate and commercial claim processes. This manifestation also includes bringing $10–15K or more into my checking account by the week of May 15 and then another $10–15K or more into my checking account by June 15 followed by $280,500 into my checking account by July 31. All private debts will be paid.

Here is the second student's goal:

My goal is to have $5,000 in wholesale sales by the end of the five-week course.

Did your eyes glaze over when reading the first goal? Did you have to read it more than once or at least read slowly so you could get a clear sense about what she wanted? In contrast, the second student was so concise that really there is nothing else that needs to be said!

Now, that said, writing a long paragraph may be just what you need to get your thoughts organized and to help you figure out what you want. If you want something from your mate or your child, for example, doesn't it help you to have your thoughts together so when you make your request both you and the other person are clear about what you want?

In summary: be respectful by writing your goal in a complete sentence. And keep in mind that you don't want your goal to have to work too hard to figure out what you want. Just like a person, your goal appreciates a to-the-point request.

GIVE YOUR GOAL A TIME FRAME

Deadlines give you something to aim for whether you are training for a marathon, planning a wedding or finishing a work project. A goal is more likely to spring into action when it has ten days to deliver than if it has an unlimited amount of time to get it done. Plus, how badly do you want it? A goal that you want to achieve soon simply has your full attention. Something that you don't care about happening today or fifty years from now won't have the oomph needed for manifestation. If you are asking your goal to go out of its way to help you, it should be important to you now!

YOUR GOAL SHOULD BE SIMPLE AND SPECIFIC

The more specific you are, the more your goal has to work with. This is true for any conversation or any relationship. For example, if your spouse asks you what you want and you say, "You should know what I want!" or "Make me happy," you are not giving your partner much to work with!

On the other hand, too much information up front can be a bit arduous for your goal. If you are on a first date, for example, and your date presents a long list of requirements that include specifics about lovemaking ability, plans for children and salary must-haves, wouldn't you think twice about seeing that person again?

Your relationship with your goal, just like with a mate or a job, will unfold over time. Pace yourself! This is not the only conversation you will ever have with your goal. In fact you will in all probability tweak and amend your goal more than once.

Here are two examples of a goal—the first has too little information and the second has too much.

First student's goal:

I want to receive a job that feeds my soul.

Second student's goal:

I want the following dream job.
Environment:
  Clean physical environment
  Bright access to windows
  Warm in winter/cool in summer
  Smart people, people I can learn from
  Fun people, people I can laugh with
  Space to spread out
  Convenient location
  Feels like home/family-like
  Company with integrity, "do the right thing"
  People are valued and treated with respect and dignity
  Hardworking but relaxed atmosphere
  A community of people working together for a good
    cause
  Room to grow and learn
  Nurturing and supportive

Benefits:
   Up to 32 hrs/week
Flexible hours
   3 weeks vacation
   Health insurance/preferably BlueCross BlueShield
   Dental insurance
Salary: $50,000 per year or more
Duties: Use my God-given gifts and talents

The first goal is too hard to figure out! If *you* are not clear, why would your goal be clear? How will your goal know what to deliver? It's not a psychic fairy godmother! Doesn't it make sense that a lack of specificity is an impediment to actualizing a goal? Many of my students find that they need to give considerable thought and time to help them state exactly what it is they want. Take your time so you can communicate clearly.

The second student has front-loaded her request with so many requirements (and interestingly without stating anything about the actual job) that her goal may move on to someone who is not so high-maintenance. Can you imagine interviewing for a job and giving the interviewer that list?

Again, this can be a great exercise on your way to writing a one-sentence goal. But let it be just that—an exercise!

DON'T GET HUNG UP ON HOW YOUR GOAL IS WORDED

If it's not spelled correctly or the grammar is incorrect and you have a double negative in your sentence, don't worry about it unless your goal is to be an English teacher. Just start the process.

Some of my students have read about the importance of stating a goal in the present tense rather than the future tense. While this can be a fun and interesting exercise, it is not necessary.

I was watching Cesar Millan's TV show *The Dog Whisperer* recently. He made the excellent point to a dog's owner that it wasn't the words but the energy behind the words that makes a dog do what you want it to do. Have you ever yelled, "sit" over and over again while your dog continues to do anything but?

If you write your goal down like this, "I want to get a job that pays me an annual salary of $100,000," your goal is not confused about what you are asking for. It is not necessary to write, "I have a job that pays me $100,000 each year." In fact, that statement all by itself can set up a little riptide of resistance since you know that is not your current salary. While manifestation occurs in the present, a word by itself does not hold that power.

The issue of past, present and future as it relates to goal manifestation is a fascinating one and I will be discussing it at length later in this book. (The previous sentence referred to the future. Once you are reading those later sections, you will be in the present. But I don't want to get ahead of myself—so, onward!)

YOUR GOAL SHOULD BE MEASURABLE

You need to know when you have actually achieved your goal. For example, if your goal is to get a job, you will know whether you have a job or you don't. If your goal is to be happy or to feel good, ask yourself how you will know that you have reached your goal. What are the results of being happy or feeling good? What does that look like?

Choose a concrete outcome. Do you want more money? A relationship? A new car? This is not the time to explore the abstract nature of happiness—does it come from within or from outside of yourself, etc. I discuss the more philosophical issues of wanting, asking and receiving later in this book. For now, just choose something that you want and that you will recognize when you receive it—and write it down in one sentence.

DON'T LIMIT YOURSELF

Don't decide ahead of time that your goal is unrealistic. Write exactly what you want. You are starting a relationship with your goal. You and the goal will work out some of the finer details as you get to know each other.

Once you write your goal down, set it aside. Don't keep fiddling with it. The reason for this is that you want your goal to communicate with you. And if you are doing all of the talking, your goal won't be able to get a word in edgewise!

You are now in a relationship with your goal. Be a good partner; be kind and considerate. Don't be high maintenance. Don't be a drama queen. Don't be a wallflower. As you become an experienced Receiver, not only will your goal easily connect with you, but also you will be able to hear (receive) what your goal is telling you.

Now that you have written down your goal, the next section describes the first steps that show you how to draw it toward you. Like a magnet.

the three steps

Accept All Compliments
Count Your Blessings
Be Spiritually Naked

Now that you have your goal's attention, your job is to create fertile soil so that it can plant itself.

These first three steps are designed to help you spend more of your energy and time in the receptive state. By doing so, you will strengthen your receiving ability, which will attract your dreams and goals to you.

I have many exercises in this book that are designed to acquaint you with your Receive Muscles. But these first three steps are the cornerstones for your Receive Practice. They are remarkably effective with consistent daily application. If you don't become adept at them, your Receive Practice will falter. By mastering them, you will find there is little that will not be yours for the asking.

Have fun and enjoy!

STEP ONE

Accept All Compliments

God has given us two hands, one to receive with and the other to give with.

—BILLY GRAHAM

Don't turn away what life wants to give to you. A huge connection exists between what you are willing to receive and what you actually get. I call this step "Accept All Compliments" because I have noticed a correlation between people's unwillingness to receive the simplest things in life, while at the same time having some pretty big expectations. Your ability to receive something as simple as a compliment is significant. It signals loud and clear that you are ready to receive.

Let's get started with a few simple rules to remember when you are complimented or helped in some way.

First, when people give you a compliment, accept it graciously. If someone says, "I love that shirt you're wearing. It looks great on you!" don't say, "This old rag? I got it at the thrift shop for fifty cents." And for heaven's sake, don't point out the stain on it!

Interestingly, one of the definitions of the word *acceptance* is "to receive willingly." When we push away or do not receive willingly, people notice! A lack of acceptance and acknowledgment sends the message loud and clear that we don't want to be given to. And life cooperates by being less giving.

"But nobody tries to give me anything!" you may think. "How am I going to get life to give to me?"

Life is constantly giving. But only Receivers notice it. So, if life gives to those who can receive, as soon as you receive, life gives. You will be absolutely amazed when you see how this actually happens. It feels miraculous.

Receiving takes practice. If you start with the smaller things, you will soon graduate to the bigger ones. Here are a few suggestions to get you started:

- Thank the grocery clerk for putting the food in the bag.
- Thank the person who tells you your eyes are beautiful.
- Thank the bank teller for saying, "Have a nice day."
- Thank the driver who waves at you to go first at the stop sign.
- Thank the waiter for bringing you coffee.

- Thank your cat for using the litter box.
- Thank your coworker for saying, "Have a great weekend."
- Thank your houseplants for their beauty.

Receive the pleasure of living in a world where people compliment you, are kind to you and are considerate of you. Be genuinely appreciative. How great is it that people will do something for you, serve you in some way, give to you? Be excited by it! Celebrate it! Life's abundance is everywhere. And the more you notice it, the more life gives.

You may be asking yourself whether just accepting compliments, kind words and gifts can help you manifest your goals. The answer is yes! Your goal cannot connect with someone who doesn't even notice it, let alone know how to receive it. And this takes practice. Think of your goal as watching you, wondering if you are a good bet, questioning if it should commit.

Here is an example of what can occur with just a little practice in receiving.

Jill had a history of being available and helpful to her coworkers. She secretly and resentfully noted that her acts of kindness were not reciprocated, but she had always attributed this to the ungrateful nature of these particular people.

During the second class of my five-week Receive and

Manifest course, she reported that the day after the first class a coworker, totally unsolicited, brought her coffee.

"This may not seem like a big deal to any of you, but in all of the years I've worked there, no one had ever done something like this," Jill said. After she recovered from the shock of having the coffee brought to her, her first impulse was to say, "Oh, you shouldn't have!" But she remembered Step One, "Accept All Compliments," and instead she graciously thanked her coworker.

That one cup of coffee, seemingly such a small gift, began a new chapter for Jill. If you start small, you, too, will begin to see the results of your Receive practice.

exercise

Here are a few exercises to practice every day:
- Look for opportunities to thank people.
- Notice any tendency you have to stop the abundant flow of the universe coming toward you by saying something like, "Oh, you didn't need to do that!"

- If you are uncomfortable with accepting a compliment, kind words or a gift, note that feeling and receive it. But still say, "Thank you."
- Keep in mind that the longer it takes you to incorporate this first step into your life, the longer it will take your goal to connect with you.

STEP TWO

Count Your Blessings

Let your heart be awakened to the transforming power of gratefulness.

—SARAH BAN BREATHNACH

To be grateful is to be receptive to life's givingness, life's abundance. Gratitude is a state of mind, a way of seeing life, of noticing and relating to life. Following are a few gratitude rules to help you strengthen your Receive Muscles.

- When you tell someone you are grateful for something they have done for you, you are not only giving them the gift of your enjoyment, but also your gratitude is likely to inspire the person to give again. It feels good to be appreciated!

- There are no degrees of gratitude. Whether you are grateful for eating breakfast in bed or for the beautiful tree outside your window, your brain just registers gratefulness. It doesn't decide that you should be more grateful for the tree than for breakfast in bed.

- It takes *you* to look for something that you can be grateful for.

There are those who have an overall attitude of gratitude. Conversely, some people are rarely grateful—even when people bend over backward to give to them.

Appreciation and gratitude come from *within* a person as a way of looking at life, as a way of being in life. It is completely independent of external circumstances.

Since gratitude is a receptive state, the more grateful you are (receiving), the more you have to be grateful for (more to receive). The concept is this:

- Gratitude is a receptive state.
- Whatever you focus on grows.
- Continual daily focus on gratitude increases your capacity to receive.
- Receivers manifest because they appreciate their goals.

exercise

Start a journal that is devoted to recording daily gratitudes. Each day record (at least) five things for which you feel grateful. Here are a few examples:

I am grateful for my morning coffee.
I am grateful for the beautiful tree in my front
    yard.
I am grateful that my husband received a job
    promotion.
I am grateful for the recommendation my
    friend gave me for a massage therapist.

(continued)

I am grateful that my sister is content in her life.

I am grateful for my home.

I am grateful that I have been feeling better.

Do you get the idea that you can never run out of things to write?

The purpose of this exercise is to not only be grateful for your more saintly qualities and fun events, but also to be grateful for your wholeness, which includes experiences that are uncomfortable or even painful. Consequently, to become an exceptional Receiver and manifest your goals quickly, include feelings and observations such as these:

I am grateful I was able to feel my grief today.

I am grateful that I am noticing how much I hide behind a mask of "togetherness."

I am grateful I wasn't home when my boyfriend called.

You may want to vary the way you write your gratitudes. Here are examples with variations for "I am grateful" or "I am thankful":

I so appreciate . . . the spirit of friendship that
    resides in people.

I feel extraordinarily blessed . . . that I live in
    such a beautiful house.

I receive with gratitude . . . my dog's love.

I totally embrace with arms wide open . . . all
    of the money that is coming my way.

Thank you for . . . listening to me when I
    needed to talk.

My heart is so full . . . for having known you.

I am filled with thanks for . . . the beautiful
    sunset I saw today.

I love the way . . . I am learning to see the
    world differently.

I sit in awe of . . . the insights and
    connections I made today.

The smile from that stranger came at just the
    right time. I am thrilled to live in such a
    generous world.

I kneel and pray in thanks for . . . this
    amazing journey.

(continued)

You may want to include a current goal in your gratitudes, writing it as if it had already manifested. Just as the brain records *gratefulness* without placing a hierarchy on what constitutes gratefulness, the brain does not recognize the feeling of gratefulness within a time framework. So, if your goal is to increase your salary and you write, *I am grateful my salary has increased so I can afford the new roof for the house,* your brain registers *gratefulness.* It's an *experience* the brain is registering.

I am going to caution you here, just as I did in the goal writing section at the beginning of this chapter, to avoid writing your goal in the present tense unless you are completely comfortable doing so. Otherwise you will create resistance, which is, of course, counterproductive.

Please don't go overboard writing your gratitudes with the expectation that the more times you write your goal, the sooner it will manifest. Remember, you are in a relationship with your goal, and being attentive and listening to your goal's feedback is important. So, don't pester your goal writing over and over again about how grateful you are! Imagine if you were to tell your boss over and over and over again how grateful you are for the raise. Your boss may reconsider giving you another one next year if you keep gushing how grateful you are! Nobody wants to be fawned over. It's annoying. Don't irritate your goal. Have a nice sense of relationship about this gratitude thing.

Summary

- Each day write down five experiences for which you are grateful.
- Make sure you write them in full sentences.
- It is important that you write them down rather than just think them. Writing them down demonstrates a much bigger commitment. Your goal will notice this.
- It doesn't matter when you write your gratitudes. You may want to create a habit of starting your day writing in your gratitude journal. Or you may want to write your gratitudes before you go to sleep. You can write them in your car while waiting at a red light.
- After you write all five gratitudes, choose one

and spend a full sixty seconds visualizing yourself in the experience of that gratitude. This is not only a relaxing and enjoyable exercise but it also strengthens your Receive Muscles. And, every time you cultivate a greater capacity to receive, your ability to manifest increases.

- Be aware that unless you have spent your life in a state of gratitude, the mind can create a powerful resistance to this exercise. For example, your mind may convince you that you don't have enough time even though the exercise itself lasts no longer than two minutes. Now, everybody can find two minutes in a day!

Over the years, I have seen the people who do this exercise daily become Receivers who manifest their dreams. Those who don't spend the time, don't. Now, that's incentive!

STEP THREE

Be Spiritually Naked

When you reveal yourself to another human being . . . you reveal yourself to God.

—Eva Pierrakos

To be spiritually naked is to be self-revealing. It means that you don't just trot out the "good," healed and healthy parts of your personality when you are with people. It means that you express all of your vulnerable, clueless, hateful, depressed, lost and lonely parts, too. You include them in your conversations with others and with yourself. The reason for this is that if you embrace your wholeness, others will also.

It's hard to relate to those who come across as if they are totally "together," enlightened human beings. Instead, we love it when people come across as being just as human as we are. It creates a bond. We feel that we are with a fellow traveler, a kindred spirit.

When we are open and honest about all of who we are, we are not only making a statement about our connection with everyone but we are also making a declaration about our wholeness.

It is a sign of strength to be authentic. It takes courage to embrace all parts of ourselves and to share them with others. Once we are comfortable with being genuine, we seek out others who are as well. It is relaxing to be in the presence of an imperfect human being.

Hiding who we are inhibits both giving and receiving. If you think about it—how can someone know how to be there for you if you have not revealed what is really going on? And how will *you* know there is something that you can do for an individual who hides behind a mask?

Spiritual nakedness doesn't mean that you don't have healthy boundaries or good judgment. Obviously, you don't tell the bank teller who asks you how you are about the tough time you had in your therapy session earlier in the day! Being self-revealing simply means being your authentic self rather than trying to give the impression of someone you think you should be.

Inclusion is a spiritual act, a receptive act. We make a statement about our wholeness when we include all of who we are. To expand your capacity to receive, look for occasions to showcase your wholeness.

exercise

Each day, seek out and take advantage of the opportunities to be self-revealing. Here are a few examples:

Friend: How are you making out with your job search?
Old You: Great!
New You: Although the interviews seem to be going well, I am worried that I am overqualified and may not find the right job match for me.

Daughter: Mom, some friends invited me to go out tonight. Will you watch the kids?
Old You: Sure! What time do you need me there?
New You: Honey, I am feeling in a really quiet mood and just want to stay home alone tonight.

Acquaintance: You are so independent! Do you prefer being single?
Old You: I don't need anyone to complete me! I'm very satisfied with my life.

(continued)

New You: I love my independent nature, but to tell you the truth, it would be wonderful to be in a relationship again.

As simple as the above statements may seem, it is amazing how often we don't reveal exactly what it is that we are experiencing or feeling. These omissions accumulate over time and become a chronic method of relating.

When we do not reveal what we are experiencing, we don't give others the chance to be there for us or to give to us. And what so often happens is that the people in your life do not consider what you may be experiencing or feeling. Here are examples:

Friend: How are you making out with your job search?

Old You: Great!

Friend concludes: She seems to be doing just fine. I was thinking of a company that would be a great fit for her, but I don't want to intrude on what seems to be working. She obviously has this handled.

Daughter: Mom, some friends invited me to go out tonight. Will you watch the kids?

Old You: Sure! What time do you need me there?

Daughter concludes: I am glad Mom is always so available and obviously enjoys spending her free time with my children. I was thinking of searching for a babysitter, but why should I when Mom loves watching the kids. This is a perfect situation! We are both getting our needs met.

Acquaintance: You are so independent! Do you prefer being single?

Old You: I don't need anyone to complete me! I'm very satisfied with my life.

Acquaintance concludes: I know someone who I think would really like her, but he is looking for a serious relationship, so I won't mention it. She seems to be very content.

When we don't reveal ourselves, life has no opportunity to give in ways that could feel rewarding, exciting and energizing.

If you feel stuck, make sure that you let people

(continued)

know that you are open to receiving ideas, support and feedback.

I love this quote by Dinah Shore: "Trouble is a part of your life, and if you don't share it, you don't give the person who loves you a chance to love you enough."

It is relaxing to be authentic. It puts others at ease. And relaxed people manifest more easily than tense, wound-up people. Spiritual nakedness is about transparency. Don't make people, your goal or *you* have to work so hard to know who you are and what you want.

No Suffering Allowed

No Suffering Aloud

no suffering allowed!
no suffering aloud!

Misery is a communicable disease.

—MARTHA GRAHAM

Can you imagine going up to someone you are interested in dating and complaining about the lack of decent men or women and that all those you meet are selfish, controlling idiots? How attractive would that be to your prospective partner? It's a great tactic to scare someone away, but not to keep him or her around!

It's the same with your goal. Why would your goal want to come near you if you are complaining about it all the time? If your goal is to meet a loving partner, you will chase it away with your cynical, judgmental, unpleasant attitude.

We live in a society where complaining is a way of life and a way to bond. On any particular day, you will hear people in an elevator, those waiting in line at the grocery store and even people walking down the street, detailing some unfairness, slight or insult. This is one of the ways we discharge energy that has built up through resentment and disappointment. However, complaining slams shut the Receiving Door.

Many of us are not aware of how often we communicate the details of our suffering, nor do we fully grasp how we drain energy from our listeners. But complaining has an additional insidious consequence—it robs us of the energy needed to achieve a goal.

FEELINGS ARE UNIVERSAL— YOUR STORY IS NOT

Complaining is different than talking about your feelings. Complaining is telling a story about your suffering with you as the victim. Feelings are universal; everyone can relate to them. Every feeling you've had has been experienced in some version by everyone else.

A story is not universal. It is specific to you. For example, if you gripe about your boss and the details of your job, your listeners will not be as attentive as they would be if you were talking about feeling unappreciated. People can relate to feeling unappreciated.

How often have you tried to get away from someone who is going on and on about their troubles, recounting in agonizing minutia the cause of their suffering? How often have you done the same thing and watched people's eyes glaze over? No one wants to be trapped listening to a mono-logue of misery!

When you express your genuine feelings, not only will others relate to you but also you will start relating to your-self. Staying in touch with your feelings instead of catalogu-ing injustices helps you to receive rather than deflect your present circumstances. When you listen to what your emo-tions are communicating, you open up the possibility of instituting changes that can be helpful to you.

Advanced Receivers don't complain, not because they try to put a stop to that impulse, but because a Receiver's focus is about receiving—not scaring away.

How do you talk about your goal? Imagine that your goal is listening to everything you say. Think of your goal as evalu-ating *you* and wondering how much it should invest in you.

If you want more money, it's not helpful to complain about it, because you want money to be attracted to you. If you long for a happy mate who wants to come home to you, you can't nitpick as soon as he or she walks through the front door. If you want your parents to be kinder to you, you can't pout and sulk and act like they are a pain to be around. If you want a better job, you can't constantly grumble about how there aren't any good jobs available.

In summary:

- Complaints push away rather than draw things toward you.
- Complaints discharge energy without changing anything.
- Complaints are about a story rather than about your feelings.

If you stop complaining, not only will your goal become attracted to you, people will, too.

exercise

Instituting a Complaint Fast is one of the most effective things you can do to strengthen your capacity to receive and therefore your ability to manifest your dreams.

Start with spending one day without complaining. If you feel ambitious, make a vow to eliminate complaints completely. The "No Suffering Allowed, No Suffering Aloud" motto on page 78 can help you. You may want to put it on your refrigerator or any other place where you will see it frequently.*

Although you are not complaining, make sure you are expressing your feelings. Your complaints are a sign that something does not feel right. Legitimize that! When you have an impulse to complain, check in with your emotions instead. Sit with them a bit. Become familiar with what they are telling you.

Speaking about your feelings doesn't mean that you delete the context of your circumstances. Instead, your experience rather than the storyline is at the core of what you are communicating. Once you get into the practice of this, you will view the conditions of your life differently, which in turn will cause you to make new choices about the circumstances you find distressing.

People who manifest their dreams are not the people who are complaining. There is a reason for that. It saps too much energy, it's counterproductive, and it's uninteresting. Join their ranks and make this your motto: *No suffering allowed! No suffering aloud!*

---

*Go to www.The PowerofReceiving.com, where you can print your own copy of this motto.

CHAPTER THREE

helping your goal

Cultivating Receiving

removing the halo

> *Our image of perfection is the reason we reject ourselves the way we are, and why we don't accept others the way they are.*
>
> —DON MIGUEL RUIZ

"*I hope after I leave a room,* people turn to each other and say, 'She is such a nice, decent, good person'!" Sandra and I burst into laughter. My friend had spent the first fifty years of life trying her best to please others. She had been talking about her past, for she had long ago let go of those shackles. No longer a prisoner of social "niceness," she was a woman unencumbered by people's opinion of her.

Why do you think it is that people become so sensitive to other people's opinions in the first place?

When you were growing up, were you rewarded for being a "good girl" or a "good boy"? How do you think you translated that statement? Probably, you simply connected the dots that your behavior had made your mom, dad, schoolteacher, or somebody else happy. They were happy with *you*. I doubt that you analyzed the specifics.

When you are a child and the adults in your environment are happy with your behavior, you receive the benefits in the form of praise, an increased feeling of security and sometimes gifts. It makes sense to a child that when the grown-ups are happy with you, life is good.

Flash forward to your adult life and add in religious and cultural philosophies that put a halo over the head of someone who gives to others and you have, well, an interesting conundrum.

Many of us are taught that a good person is someone who gives to others and places the needs of others before his or her own. While there's nothing wrong with being a giving person—in fact, giving should be encouraged—when it becomes an expectation instead of a choice, we can easily become identified with the "good person" role, whether or not there is an actual desire to give. The thought that goes with this role is: I *should* do something, rather than I *want* to do something.

I am not advocating the idea that we should not give unless or until we are totally on board. Instead, I am exploring the constraints of a social role that actually inhibits giving.

Do you agree with any of the following statements?

- A good mother places her child's desires above her own.
- A good husband provides for his family.
- A good employee stays late at the office when her boss requests it.
- A good daughter does what her mother asks.
- A good son eats Sunday dinners with his mother.
- A good Christian goes to church every week.

What's wrong with the above statements? The answer is: Nothing! Nothing at all!

- Nothing, *unless* you chronically deny your own wishes and desires

- Nothing, *unless* you feel guilty if you say no to people's requests
- Nothing, *unless* you want to say *no*—but can't
- Nothing, *unless* you habitually reject your needs to the point that you don't even know what they are anymore
- Nothing, *unless* your desire to not upset others overrides what you want
- Nothing, *unless* you don't know how to set appropriate boundaries
- Nothing, *unless* you are motivated by *should* instead of *want to*
- Nothing, *unless* you rarely or never share your needs and desires
- Nothing, *unless* the important people in your life never know your true feelings

Why would anyone not take his or her own needs into account? For many, taking care of oneself is considered selfish, especially if somebody could benefit by your time, attention and help. And being a "selfish person" is a *major* fear of many people. As one of my students put it, "I'm okay if people don't think of me as a good person, but I'll do anything to avoid being viewed as a selfish person!"

The belief that a good person thinks less about his or her own needs than those of others leads people to create competing agendas. For example, one thought is, "I deserve a relationship with a giving person." The other thought (often subconscious) is, "Being a good person means that you give to others and consider their needs more than your own."

It's like the old vaudeville entertainers who, when people applauded their performance, would hold out one hand in the stop signal, while the other hand beckoned for more applause.

Due to societal expectations, men and woman typically adopt roles according to gender, with men being the Providers and women the Caregivers. In spite of social respect for and even the seeming virtue of these roles, the reality is that many feel the painful consequences of being identified with them.

Feeling that our needs are valued within a context of fulfilling someone else's needs places us in the untenable position of submerging, making unimportant or sublimating desires that we have for ourselves that are not supported by others.

What happens when you are locked into a "good person" role? Here are some of the possibilities:

- You are drained from upholding this image
  due to rescuing, saving, helping and looking
  after other people's needs at the expense of your
  own.
- You feel resentful or angry.
- You take out your frustrations on the least empowered people in your environment.
- You turn to unhealthy substances, food or activities as a way to "give" to yourself.

What does this have to do with attaining your dreams and goals? If you feel like your needs are less important than those of others, you will continually set up life situations in which your needs are not considered. If *you* do not see your needs as important, why would your goal perceive you as being an ideal choice for manifesting its desire? You have already told yourself and everyone else that you are a "good person" whose needs are less important than the desires of others!

This is what you may be broadcasting:

- If your goal is to get a better job, there is someone else who is a better candidate than you.
- If your goal is to attract a great relationship partner, that wonderful person will be attracted to

someone else—the one whose desires are more important than yours.

- If you want to increase your income, money will find someone who doesn't feel that someone else could use it more than you.

The bottom line is if you exclude yourself, life will cooperate by setting you to the side. Challenge your thinking in this area and revise your ideas about what it means to be a good person. Help your goal by redefining a "good person" as a "whole person." Because halo removal is so essential to goal manifestation, the following sections explore this subject further.

letting go of the punishment/reward paradigm

There is nothing good or bad, but thinking makes it so.
—WILLIAM SHAKESPEARE

"Life is difficult," M. Scott Peck writes in the opening line of *The Road Less Traveled*.

"Life is suffering," is the first of the Buddha's Four Noble Truths.

"Life is not fair," writes Rabbi Harold S. Kushner in *When Bad Things Happen to Good People*.

Although it is clear that the world does not operate on a reward/punishment model in which good people always have good things happen to them while the wicked are justly punished, beliefs persist that the world should reward the righteous and punish the evildoer.

It's worth bearing in mind that notions of good and bad depend on one's religion, culture and personal values. Are you acting from a belief about what defines a good person? Are you drawing from a personal philosophy that doesn't give you wiggle room to be human?

Here are a few funny quotes that challenge ideas of good and bad:

It has been my experience that folks who have no vices have very few virtues.

—ABRAHAM LINCOLN

Sin is a dangerous toy in the hands of the virtuous. It should be left to the congenitally sinful, who know when to play with it and when to let it alone.

—H. L. MENCKEN

Whenever I'm caught between two evils, I take the one I've never tried.

—MAE WEST

It is absurd to divide people into good or bad. People are either charming or tedious.

—OSCAR WILDE

My good intentions are completely lethal.

—MARGARET ATWOOD

Revise old ideas of bad and good to help you open up to receive.

receiving is spiritual

The difference between a helping hand and an out-stretched palm is a twist of the wrist.

—LAURENCE LEAMER

Receiving is much harder than giving. It can be emotionally risky; it requires opening up to a possibility or desire that may not be fulfilled. Giving is easy. Not only do you get to showcase your more saintly qualities but also your ego enjoys the reward—the payoff of giving.

Some time ago, when I was searching for ideas about the benefits of receiving, I read a short story about monks who were living in the Himalayas. These men, after years of religious training, were asked to go down into the streets and beg for alms. That was the whole story.

Although this is not an unusual sight in countries where Buddhism is an integral part of the culture, I wondered what it would take to do this simple act here in the West. I thought about the homeless people in my country and how people turn their heads away so they don't have to see them. I thought about the shame that so many of the destitute feel and about the judgment that so many express when they witness it. When begging, one thing is clear—there is no room for the ego. In fact, you'd have to put your ego to the side.

The more I thought about this story, the more I thought of receiving as a spiritual act and of begging for alms as a declaration of unity—that the Giver and the Receiver are one—that we are all in this together.

Have you experienced the pleasure of giving to a grateful recipient? Isn't it obvious in that moment that receiving and giving are flip sides of the same coin? Think of yourself as a monk with a bowl, ready to receive love, kindness, respect and affection. Think of your goal as that person who wants to honor you and give to you.

Your goal has information for you. Your goal wants to help you. Your goal wants to be received. Will you put your ego to the side? Will you step outside of cultural rules and roles and your own misconceptions? Will you open your hands and turn your palms up?

You are not doing this by yourself. All of the help, information and abundance in the universe cannot get through to you if you have a negative belief about receiving. Nothing can get through that distortion. That energy is strong! It is like an energy wave that pushes away the very thing that is trying to assist! Perhaps you know people who reject again and again offers of assistance, of love, of connection. Perhaps this is you.

Help your goal and help yourself by seeing receiving as an act of generosity that demonstrates your wholeness and your connection with others.

the unity principle includes *you*

No man is an island, entire of itself; every man is a piece of the continent.

—JOHN DONNE

Can you imagine being encouraged by adults throughout your childhood to let them know whenever you felt weak, vulnerable, jealous or hateful and then praising you for having the courage to express those feelings? Emotions need acknowledgment—to be received. We pay a high price when we ignore or suppress them.

Accepting and receiving your feelings are not the same as giving permission to stay mired in them. You are simply recognizing that they are a part of being human. Years ago, I saw the Dalai Lama being interviewed. He was asked if he ever felt anger. He laughed as he said, "Of course!" He explained that an emotion, just like an ocean wave, once experienced, returns to the ocean. In the same way, he said, you experience the emotion, but don't get stuck there; it returns to the source.

Just as a feeling needs inclusion, you do, too! Do you exclude and think of yourself as the "helper" to everybody else as if others are worthy and you aren't? Although you are an important, integral part of the whole shebang—the universe, the world, your community, your family, your relationships, it is *you* who must include yourself. It's no one else's job! Here are statements that can indicate you are excluding yourself:

- Oh, don't worry about me. I can handle it.
- Go out! I'll stay here and watch the kids.
- She has enough to handle. I'll stay late and do the work.
- Don't worry about the dishes. Go enjoy yourself. I'll clean up.

Here are statements that can demonstrate you are including yourself:

- Thanks for your offer of assistance. I really appreciate it.
- I'd love the help! Thanks for watching the kids.
- The work will be here when we come in tomorrow. Let's take a break.
- You dry; I'll wash.

WHATEVER WE DON'T INCLUDE, WE MARRY, GO TO WORK FOR OR GIVE BIRTH TO

The larger concept of unity is also expressed within one person. A unified personality is one in which all parts of the self are included. Everybody has difficult, unhealed parts along with the many components of the personality that are healed, valued and easy to embrace.

What happens to the scared, clueless parts in adulthood? Where do they go? Disowned aspects of the personality don't disappear because they are ignored, just as people don't disappear because we refuse to acknowledge them! In fact, those traits we refuse to recognize in ourselves, we are inevitably drawn to in someone else. My saying *Whatever we don't include, we marry, go to work for, or give birth to* describes this phenomenon.

The psychologist Carl Jung coined the term *shadow*. The shadow represents those personality characteristics that are difficult for us to see in ourselves while being extremely easy to see in others. Jung speaks about the importance of integrating these disowned parts as a pathway to wholeness.

Receiving and embracing all aspects of who we are not only prevents us from becoming involved in unhealthy relationships but it is also a powerful expression of self-love. It takes strength to admit to ourselves and to others that we possess a myriad of traits—not just the ones we showcase to impress people. In fact, receiving all of who we are attracts us to those who not only accept but even love us for all the parts of our humanity.

Years ago, I saw an interview with Michael J. Fox. When the conversation turned to how he met his wife and what drew him to her, I was interested to hear him say that part of his attraction to her were her idiosyncrasies. "It made her interesting," he said.

As you receive all parts of yourself without judgment, your goal will come closer to you. Think of it this way:

- If you think *I can't have a relationship unless I lose weight*, your goal can't come near you because you have set up a barrier, a criteria, a requirement. Yet, there is not a universal law that dictates that people who weigh more than they would prefer can't have a relationship!

- If you think *I can't get a better job because there are no well-paying jobs in the area where I live*, you've sent out a message to your goal that your desire cannot be fulfilled. Unless you have personally spoken to everyone within the radius of your job search, this cannot be an accurate statement!

Neither people nor goals can come close to someone who isn't open to receiving them. Make it easy for your goal to move toward you, or it may conclude that helping you will require too much effort and decide to move on to someone else.

do you know what you want?

A lot of people are afraid to say what they want. That's why they don't get what they want.

—MADONNA

When I began teaching my Receive and Manifest course, I was amazed by the number of people who were unable to articulate what they wanted. It was the first time I understood that not knowing what you want is a symptom of not knowing how to receive. When you think about it, how *can* you know? How are any ideas or desires going to get through to you if your metaphorical gate doesn't swing toward you (in receiving), only away from you (in giving)?

Is it easy for you to state at some length what you *don't* want? Does your mind get fuzzy when someone asks you what you want? Do you speak in vague concepts rather than specifics?

Here are some of the reasons you may not know what you want:

- You have decided that the needs of others are more important than yours and have consequently lost awareness of your own desires.
- Most of your energy is invested in others, leaving little, if any, for you.
- You believe that a good person thinks of others more than oneself.
- You excel in the activities in the Active States word list, while not spending enough time in the receptive states listed in Receptive States word list.
- You don't have enough guilt-free practice in wanting something.
- You haven't included yourself in the world, so the world hasn't included you.
- You are afraid of appearing selfish or greedy.

Opening up to your desires is like exercising a muscle. It takes time, attention and intention. Even though wanting something for yourself is as natural as wanting something for someone else, you may need to work though uncomfortable feelings. Or you may have to challenge an attitude of, "What's the use! I won't get it anyway!" Disappointment is natural when you ask for something and don't get it. You may need to simply cultivate the ability to sit with disappointment.

Asking for anything invites the risk of rejection—which is totally okay! Getting everything you ask for can't be your objective. No healthy relationship is about getting everything you want. If it is, you'll never ask for anything unless you can predict the outcome. The point of asking is to become comfortable with not only stating your needs, but also with the fact that you *do* have needs.

Once you have asked, can you trust that the answer may come in a guise that you least expect? The story about the family, the rowboat and the helicopter discussed in chapter 1 is a great reminder that prayers and requests are answered in many different and often surprising ways. If we don't ask, we never get the chance to experience the mysterious, synchronistic and magical ways in which life speaks to us.

To desire something is natural. Take the time to figure out what you want. Be specific. Once you know, you will be able to ask for it.

cinderella's wish

"I want to go to the ball!"

In a unified universe, no thing and no one is separate; there is no division between the self and others. The miracle of Cinderella's wish is that she broke out of the victim role of catering to and sweeping up after her wicked stepmother and stepsisters. She made a wish; she wanted to go to a dance; she wanted a great dress. She included herself in her vision of the world. She didn't make herself or her desire less important than those of her stepsisters. I love the miracle that manifested from her wish to go to the ball—a fairy godmother who shows up to help her.

This is an area where many of us get stuck. We feel that we cannot make a personal wish for ourselves unless we include at the same time, for example, a wish for the end of hunger or homelessness. However, this is an artificial distinction that separates you from others. When you think about it—can you wish effectively for world peace if you are unable to make a wish for yourself?

Interestingly, Cinderella's desire to go to a dance not only changed her own life, but it also transformed the lives of those around her. Her stepmother and stepsisters, as well as the prince and the kingdom itself, all flourished through the circumstances that evolved from that one wish.

exercise

Send Cinderella to Rehab

Find a quiet place where you can be alone. Write three pages of *I want* [fill in the blank], *I want* [fill in the blank], *I want* [fill in the blank]. This is not the place to write about your desire for peace and goodwill throughout the universe or about your wish that all children have good homes. You already know that you want those things. This is an exercise of self-discovery, of finding out what you want for yourself.

(continued)

This is the place to include *you* in your vision for the world.

Another purpose of this exercise is to get out in front of the "sting" of being human. It's to give a voice to the parts that are not showcased—those that exist in you and every other human being. So, the greedier and grabbier your *I wants*, the better!

Here's an example:

> *I want to have $5 million deposited into my bank account. I want to have my very own chef who lives in a cottage on my estate, so any time I want great food it is prepared for me. I want an Olympic-size swimming pool, so I can swim daily and throw fabulous pool parties. I want a second home on an island. I want to be so beautiful that a hush falls over any room I walk into. I want a fabulous wardrobe with my own stylist to help me put it all together. I want a black Mercedes convertible and a motorcycle. I want everybody to treat me respectfully at all times. I want a confident, secure, wealthy, spiritual, emotionally mature, gorgeous*

boyfriend, who is devoted to my happiness and who wants to marry me if I want to marry him. I want everybody who has ever hurt me to write me a sincere apology letter. I want my family members to feel ecstatically grateful that I am a part of the family and to not be shy about telling me so! I want my book to be a best seller. I want to be on Oprah.

I like to think of this exercise as clearing debris out of a hose. The parts you feel guilty, geeked-out, weirded-out or embarrassed about are the debris holding everything else back.

Are you having a hard time getting started? In one of my workshops when people were feeling stumped about how to begin, I asked: "Would any of you like to eat anything you want and still have perfect health and not gain any weight? If so, start with that!" After the laughter, all the participants began scribbling in their notebooks.

If you felt repulsed when you read the above list of *I wants* and wonder how anybody could be so shallow, or

(continued)

if you think, "I don't want to write a list. I have everything I need," I'd like you to write in your journal for a bit. Have you ever in your entire life wanted something that you didn't get? Start there; build from there.

When you write your *I wants*, you are clearing out all of the bits and parts that prevent your life force from flowing out and flowing in. So include everything! I want you to have more crayons in the box; I want a bigger, richer palette for you to draw on and draw from. I want your humanity; I want your wholeness.

After you finish writing your *I wants*, if you would like to burn those pages—by all means, do so. But while you are doing it, give yourself fully to this exercise. Have fun with it! On the other side of this exercise is clarity.

deepening your relationship with your goal

*Strengthening Your
Capacity to Receive*

the big circle

> *You must live in the present, launch yourself on every
> wave, find your eternity in each moment.*
>
> —HENRY DAVID THOREAU

"*I was thinking about looking* for another job. Out of the blue, I got a call from a former boss with an interesting job offer!"

"The last thing in the world I was looking for was a

relationship, and out of the blue I met a man at the grocery store who later became my husband."

"I wanted to buy something I couldn't afford, and out of the blue someone sent me a check for $500 in appreciation for work I'd done as a favor."

"The memory of an old college friend popped into my mind yesterday, and then out of the blue I received a phone call from her today."

Just what is *that blue space* we refer to when something occurs in an unexpected or surprising way? Lisa, a participant in one of my Receive and Manifest courses, recounted the following story:

"An appliance repair guy, while fixing my old Maytag dishwasher, told me about a Bosch dishwasher, a brand I had never heard of before. Out of the blue, my husband, who hates to part with money, called to say he had just bought a Bosch dishwasher, although we had not discussed it previously and it is uncharacteristic for him to make a purchase of this kind without discussion."

I think of this "out of the blue" space as our connection to and being a part of Oneness—the place where everything and everyone is included. I call this the Big Circle or the

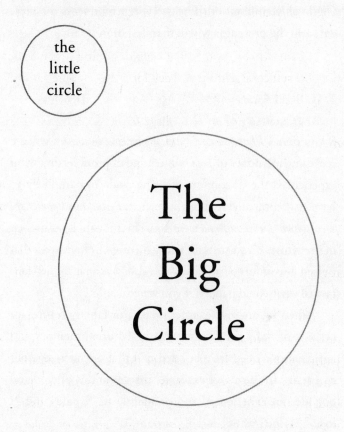

the little circle

The Big Circle

The Suffering Past ➔⟵ *The Fantasy Future*

The Pleasurable Past ➔⟵ *The Anxious Future*

Circle of Manifestation. The Big Circle represents the present, and the present is where manifestation occurs.

THE SUFFERING PAST/FANTASY FUTURE PARADIGM

If you think, *I hate winter! I am always cold in winter*, you are retrieving memories of past winters and of previous times you experienced the discomfort of being cold. You are likely to have an accompanying thought such as, *I would be happier if I were warm. I wish summer were here.* This thought is positioned in the future. If you are retrieving a memory from the past that caused discomfort or suffering, you also have an imagined fantasy of what could happen if you weren't suffering.

When we are in the suffering past or fantasy future, we operate out of a time line that is based upon memory and anticipation. They are a bonded pair that operates together as a team. In the above example, the sensations of cold and hot are not experienced independently of "I hate" and "I love," "I don't want" and "I do want."

When a goal is about being rescued from your current suffering circumstances, you are in the suffering past/fantasy future paradigm and will not manifest from this state. Here are examples:

- Pamela's fantasy to marry a wealthy man who would take care of her was directly related to working at a job she hated. *This fantasy not only makes her vulnerable to choosing inappropriate relationships, but it also diverts her from addressing her present work conditions.*

- Marlene's fantasy of winning the lottery was directly related to her anxiety about her subsistence-level income. *This fantasy not only makes her vulnerable to gambling away what little money she has, but it also distracts her from seeking out new moneymaking opportunities.*

- Richard's fantasy of making a lot of money while doing little work was related to his current job where he worked excessive hours at a job he found unrewarding. *This fantasy not only makes him vulnerable to a get-rich-quick scheme but it also sidetracks him from actively perusing more suitable employment.*

A fantasy is a discharge mechanism that is directly related to your past and keeps you tethered to your current condition.

THE PLEASURABLE PAST/ANXIOUS FUTURE PARADIGM

Just as the suffering past is connected to the fantasy future, the pleasurable past is connected to the anxious future. When we are in this time line, we are concerned that the future may not replicate the happy memories from the past.

Here are a few examples:

- Ann excelled in her studies in high school. *She worries that she will not do as well in college.*
- Mark was such a precocious child that grown-ups sought out his advice. *As an adult he worries about maintaining his importance.*
- Laura grew up being told she was beautiful and talented enough to be a movie star. *As an adult, she feels anxious when she is not the center of attention.*

The Big Circle represents the present. It is completely separate from memories of the past and anticipations about the future. It is what is here right now. When you don't retrieve anything from the past, there is no compare-and-contrast mechanism. In the example about winter, the experience of cold has no accompanying evaluation or judgment. It just *is*.

How do we enter the Big Circle and utilize it to obtain our goals? Quantum theory offers clues through the ideas of local and nonlocal space and particles and waves. Simply, local space is where you are right now and nonlocal space is everywhere else. While the woman in the earlier story thought about a Bosch dishwasher she wanted, her husband was actually buying it. Nonlocal space is that link or information that was accessed by husband and wife. They were not in each other's physical presence or even connected by telephone. Nor had they had a previous conversation about the dishwasher—all of which would be local space. Basically, both received the *idea* of the Bosch dishwasher that was floating in the Big Circle.

While all energy and information is in the Big Circle, it takes an observer to particle-ize specific information or energy. Until the wife thinks about the dishwasher, the idea of the *dishwasher* is simply floating around in the Big Circle as an energy idea wave that doesn't really land anywhere. It needs the person to bring it into existence, to particle-ize it, to concretize it through her attention to a Bosch dishwasher.

Here's the interesting part. Which came first? Was it the wife's desire for the Bosch dishwasher or the husband's purchase? The answer is neither.

The Big Circle operates outside time and space; it *is* the

present. The idea or information energy bundle is in the Big Circle, and both husband and wife are observers of the idea of the Bosch dishwasher. After it is installed and neither is observing it anymore, the idea is still in the Big Circle. It hasn't disappeared. It hasn't gone anywhere. It's an energy wave again. But each time they bring their attention to *Bosch dishwasher*, they particle-ize it again. When their attention is elsewhere, it's an energy wave again.

PARTICLE-IZING YOUR GOAL

How can you particle-ize your goal? Anything and everything exists in the Big Circle. Your goal requires an observer to bring it into manifestation. Prior to that, it is only an energy-humming bundle of information, potential and possibility. In other words, your goal connects with you once *you* form a relationship to it. (Or has your goal particle-ized *you*?) Regardless, entering the Big Circle is the prerequisite for manifesting your goal.

Receptivity is an experience of the present and the Big Circle represents the present. So, the more time you spend receiving, the more quickly you manifest your dreams, desires and goals. Here are the previously discussed exercises that gain you entrance into the Big Circle:

- Accepting compliments
- Writing gratitudes
- Being spiritually naked
- Experiencing any one of the states
  in the Receptive States word list
- Not complaining

Now that we have a sense of the Big Circle, it is time to shed light on the Little Circle.

the little circle

He drew a circle that shut me out—
Heretic, rebel, a thing to flout.
But Love and I had the wit to win:
We drew a circle that took him in.

—EDWIN MARKHAM

The Little Circle exists separate from and outside of the Big Circle. Anything and everything you have cast out of the Big Circle resides in this Little Circle. Remember, the Big Circle represents Oneness; it's where you experience your connection with everything.

Little Circle
Inhabitants

vegetarians

fat   pessimism

ugly

clean   lazy   good   politicians

short   sad   depression

anger   shy

drama queens   critics   martyrs   dogs

educated   lawyers

do-gooders   happy   optimism

Democrat   Virgos   thin   blue collar

bad   young   doctors   meat-eaters

dirty   sinner

beautiful   big   tall   bully   single

old   rich   candy   poor

people who don't cry

cats   Scorpios   married   saint

people who cry   short

Republicans

The Little Circle is firmly fixed in time and space and is related to our suffering past/fantasy future and pleasurable past/anxious future. It is a repository for all disowned, unacknowledged and uncomfortable bits and parts. The Little Circle holds everything we don't include. It contains everything we throw out of the Big Circle, such as feelings we don't embrace, people we look down on or up to, or ideas we dismiss.

Here are examples of what you may have placed into the Little Circle:

Fat, thin, bad, good, ugly, beautiful, short, tall, young, old, happy, sad, optimism, pessimism, dogs, cats, single, married, clean, dirty, big, small, rich, poor, saint, sinner, lawyers, doctors, politicians, educated, blue collar, Virgos, Scorpios, drama queens, martyrs, critics, lazy people, do-gooders, people who cry, people who don't cry, vegetarians, meat-eaters.

Everything in the Little Circle:

- Inhibits manifestation of your goals
- Runs your life from behind the scenes, from the subconscious

- Behaves like a maverick with its own agenda
- Interferes with what you want

Here is an example:

You know you don't want to eat the ice cream in the freezer because you are trying to lose weight. The entire time you are thinking this, you walk to the kitchen, open the freezer door, take out the ice cream, get a spoon and eat what's left of the ice cream.

What is it that makes you go for the ice cream even though you know you want to avoid it? The Little Circle is the voice that says: *What's the use in stopping yourself? You know you'll just eat it eventually anyway.* It's the voice that says: *Eat it now and then it won't be there tomorrow when you really start your diet.*

Here is another example:

You have a deadline to complete a work project, and as much as you want to get to it, you keep noticing other things like the bathtub that needs cleaning, fingernails that need clipping and dust on the top of the doors that needs vacuuming.

This maverick that sabotages what you consciously know you want resides in the Little Circle. What does this insistent rebel want?

INCLUSION

Have you ever been to a party where you knew few, if any, people and stood by yourself, feeling awkward while you watched them chatting and having a good time? Or, in a situation like this, has someone mercifully come over to you, talked with you and introduced you to others to help you feel comfortable?

Perhaps you've played this role yourself, helping someone to feel included. It's a relief, isn't it? You're grateful when someone reaches out to you and it's a great feeling to be that person for someone else. Everything and everyone in the Little Circle also wants to be included. They want to come to the party and be welcomed and know that their company is desired.

There's a saying that a person reviews the faults of the one who keeps him waiting. It is common to dislike people who won't let you join in, who don't want you. It's the same with your disowned, disliked parts. They start to have a dim opinion of you and then cause trouble by impeding your growth or undermining you.

Consider this: If several hungry children came to your home for dinner, would you send those you didn't like around to the backyard to eat scraps from the garbage can

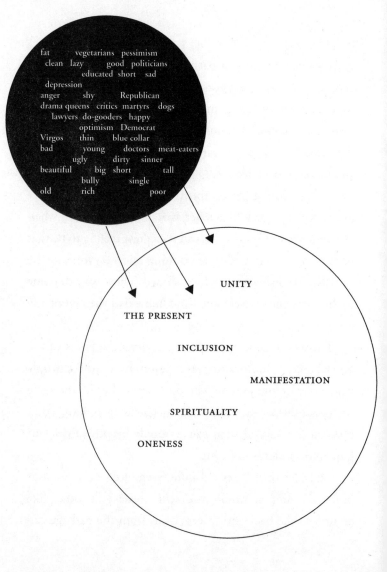

while you welcomed those you liked into your home to sit at your dinner table? What do you think would be the attitude of those you denied entrance? What would they be saying about you while they rummaged through your trash looking for food?

In our outer environment or in our interior world, those who are cast out don't actually *go* anywhere. They hang around. After all, where would they go?

A country's outcasts are terrorists. Your external outcasts are people who do things like talk behind your back. Your internal outcasts operate clandestinely from within as your very own saboteurs. They are all one and the same.

Everybody wants to be treated well. Everybody wants to be in the Big Circle. No one wants to be banished into the Little Circle, whether they are members of a family, of a country, of a world or parts of your personality. When outcasts are not welcomed, they make themselves known. They get your attention.

To help your goal help *you*, invite, include, welcome, celebrate and embrace everything. You can decide later what to do with them.

exercise

Who or what is your outcast? Who or what do you exclude? Is it anger, sadness, cluelessness or optimism? Is it your mother-in-law, your brother, a coworker or your boss?

When everything is in the Big Circle, we have a lot to work with. If *happiness* and *sadness* are in the Big Circle, we have both at our disposal and are more likely to make an appropriate choice. If, for example, anger is in the Little Circle, it will operate from behind the scenes. Consequently, we will be easily irritated or attracted to bullies. If it is in the Big Circle along with *peacefulness*, we are empowered to decide whether we want to be angry or peaceful.

Spend a day inviting everyone—global, external and internal—into your personal sphere in some way, even if only in your mind. Make decisions about them later. You don't have to be their best friend. For now, just receive them.

If you are a Democrat, invite a Republican.

If you are a socialist, invite a capitalist.

If you are in charge, invite someone not in charge.

If you are an achiever, invite laziness.

If you are an optimist, invite pessimism.

If you are a happy person, invite sadness.

If you are unhappy, invite joy.

Here are examples:

Good girl	↔	Bad boy
Miss Perfect	↔	Messed-up
God's emissaries	↔	God's fallen
Overachieving parents	↔	Slacker children
Workaholic boss	↔	Lazy employees
Clean freak	↔	Slob
Miser	↔	Spendthrift

Whatever we don't include in the Big Circle, we marry, go to work for or give birth to.

(continued)

It takes a lot of energy to keep things in the Little Circle. We have to keep an eye on them because we don't trust them or we are repulsed or fearful of them—whether or not we have married, gone to work for, or given birth to them.

All Little Circle feelings, thoughts, ideas and people will show up somewhere. When we make them conscious, we have the power to decide what to do and how to think about them. We can choose how to transform or heal them. Inviting our Little Circle exiles into the Big Circle gives us unlimited possibilities and infinite options. Spend a day with *inclusion* as your goal and watch your life change dramatically.

Every time you bring something out of the Little Circle and move it into the Big Circle, you reclaim your wholeness and your power. *Including* means just that—include. You don't have to do anything with it. You don't have to make a decision about it. You don't have to act on anything.

RECEIVE EVERYTHING—DECIDE LATER

Have an uncomfortable feeling? Don't Little-Circle it—include it.

Otherwise, that feeling runs you from behind the scenes, and it's all you'll think about.

Have an urge to eat every cookie in the bag? Don't Little-Circle it—include it.

Otherwise that urge runs you from behind the scenes and those cookies are all you'll think about.

Have an impulse to criticize someone? Don't Little-Circle it—include it.

Otherwise criticism runs you from behind the scenes and it's all you'll think about.

Invite and welcome the feelings, the urges, the cookies and the criticism into the Big Circle where they can hang out with everything else. They'll transform—and so will you.

CHAPTER FIVE

investing in your goal

Exercising Your Receive Muscles

breathing in . . . and out . . .

Breathing in, I know I am breathing in.
Breathing out, I know I am breathing out.

—THICH NHAT HANH

Someone once told me: When you pray, you ask, and when you meditate, you listen. It is a nice example of giving and receiving. Meditation quiets the mind, opening up the possibility to receive insight, guidance and relaxation. Meditation places you in the present—not in the suffering past or the fantasy future.

The following exercise in mindfulness can help you focus your attention on the present moment.*

exercise

Bring your awareness to your breath. As you breathe in, say to yourself silently: *Breathing in, I know I am breathing in.* As you breathe out, say silently to yourself: *Breathing out, I know I am breathing out.* If you have time, repeat this at least ten times. If you are pressed for time, repeat it five times. Longer gives you a little more bang for your buck. But don't wait until you have a leisurely afternoon to do it!

This exercise keeps your mind in the present by giving it a job to do while you are breathing. This helps you stay in the present. And, every time you are in the present, you strengthen your Receive Muscles, which in turn strengthens your capacity to manifest. Remember, all manifestation occurs in the present.

(continued)

*This exercise is from Thich Nhat Hanh.

You do not need to go to an ashram to do this exercise. You can do it anywhere. Here are a few possibilities:

- At work when you are put on hold during a telephone call
- In your car sitting at a red light
- During a commercial while you are watching TV
- At a family gathering when people are getting on your nerves
- Waiting in the line at the grocery store
- Waiting for your boyfriend to answer your question
- Waiting for your girlfriend to be ready to walk out the door

These are all potent times for your mind to wander into the suffering past and fantasy future.

There are many advantages to focusing on your breathing including the following. Notice that the receptive states below are words from the Receptive States list in chapter 1.

- It helps you know what you are feeling.
  (Feeling is a receptive state.)
- It increases your awareness of those in your
  environment. (Awareness is a receptive state.)
- It relaxes you. (Relaxation is a receptive state.)
- It gives you the experience of allowing life
  to be your partner, rather than trying to
  control life. (Allowing is a receptive state.)
- It reminds you that life is about receiving as
  well as giving. (Receiving is a receptive state.)

Now, let's take this exercise in another direction.

Breathe in something you like about yourself.

Think of something you like about yourself. Now,
breathe that thought in and out, repeating silently:

Breathing in, I'm breathing in [say your word or
phrase here], something I like about myself.
Breathing out, I'm breathing out [say your word or
phrase here], something I like about myself.

(continued)

Do this in-breath and out-breath at least ten times.

Here are some of the qualities you may like about yourself:

- Compassionate
- Sense of humor
- Gutsy
- Conscientious
- Friendly
- Kind
- Smart

You can probably relate to all of the above. They may not be on your top-ten list, but throughout your lifetime, you have experienced a version of all of them. This is because these traits are universal. All are in the Big Circle. There isn't a feeling, quality or experience that you've had, no matter how small, that isn't available to everyone else.

Now let's do this exercise a little differently.

Breathe in something you don't like about yourself.

Think of something you *don't* like about yourself and breathe it in and out, repeating silently:

*Breathing in, I'm breathing in [say your word or
    phrase here], something I don't like about myself.
Breathing out, I'm breathing out [say your word or
    phrase here], something I don't like about myself.*

Do this in-breath and out-breath at least ten times. Here are some of the things you may not like about yourself:

- Lazy
- Insecure
- Arrogant
- Envious
- Judgmental
- Impatient

Since feelings are universal, it is likely that all of these emotions and behaviors, in some version, are familiar to you. Note if you feel uncomfortable breath-

(continued)

ing in something you dislike about yourself. Don't stop breathing it in though! Simply receive the discomfort. This is likely a new experience since we are not educated to be comfortable with or accept that we have these kinds of feelings—let alone breathe them in!

You will find that if you stay with this exercise, those feelings will dissipate and breathing in and out something you dislike about yourself will not have any "charge," nor will you experience uneasiness. For many people this shift occurs within a minute or two when they discover that it feels okay to have something that you don't like about yourself.

Conversely, some people feel resistance to breathing in something they like about themselves. If you have been taught that it is unseemly or even boastful to admit that you have traits that you like about yourself, breathing those in may feel uncomfortable. Just as with the disliked traits, continuing to breathe them in and out will help you accept and include those perfectly natural feelings.

It takes energy to push away an uncomfortable

feeling and, paradoxically, that suppression does not make the feeling go away—it makes it stronger!

Not only is it an acknowledgment of your humanity to embrace all of your experiences and feelings, but in addition, when everything is in the Big Circle (which is what this exercise facilitates), you can pick and choose the experiences you would like to have.

When feelings are disowned (I *never* feel that way!), they end up in the Little Circle. And remember Little Circle feelings:

- Run you from behind the scenes (You know you want that dessert!)
- Become shadow figures (Why are arrogant jerks always attracted to me?!)
- Make you obsess about those qualities in others (It makes me sick to see how lazy she is!)
- Show up in the people you marry, go to work for, or give birth to (My boss is so impatient!)

(continued)

Not only people have Big Circle and Little Circle feelings. Countries have them, too. If a country considers itself to be "all good" or the "best in the world," then "bad, evil" countries will be Little Circle mavericks. If a country prides itself on being difficult and badly behaved, then "virtuous, noble" countries will be the proverbial thorn in their side.

When all feelings are received into the Big Circle, you have more energy and choices available to you. For now, you may want to include both *acceptance* and *nonacceptance*, as you work to integrate and receive the full array of your feelings.

receiving and listening

Hearing is one of the body's five senses. But listening is an art.
—FRANK TYGER

"You haven't heard a word I said!"

How familiar is that statement, whether you are on the giving or receiving end? What person has never been accused of not listening? Talking to someone who is not receiving what you are saying is frustrating!

An inability to listen interferes in all of your relationships. It breaks the connection just like when a cell phone call is dropped. Or it's like having static on the line when you are trying to have a conversation.

Imagine chatting on the phone with only the receiver component working or only the part that you talk into. How unsatisfying! You would think, *What's the point of talking if I can't hear the other person?* or, *What's the point of just listening if they can't hear what I have to say?*

It's clear we need both parts for a mutually satisfying experience. It's the talking and listening together that is fun, interesting and satisfying.

There are all sorts of reasons that can interfere with the capacity to receive what someone is communicating. Here are some:

- You may assume there is no value in what someone is telling you.
- You may refuse to listen because you don't feel that *you* are listened to.
- You may not listen because you feel criticized.
- You may not listen because you haven't devel-

oped the habit of giving someone your undivided attention.
- You may feel that if you listen, the other person
  will never stop talking.
- You may think that you have all the answers and
  that nobody can tell you something you don't
  already know.
- You may feel that you'll never get your turn to
  talk.
- You may feel that you can't emotionally handle
  what someone wants to tell you.
- You may feel that if you listen to someone, you'll
  have to do whatever he or she asks.

There are many reasons that lead people to be poor listeners. If you have been told that you do not listen, review
the above list.

Talking and listening go together. Talking is giving information; listening is receiving information.

your senses are an entranceway

*We must not allow the clock and the calendar to blind
us to the fact that each moment of life is a miracle and
mystery.*

—H. G. WELLS

Our everyday environment offers numerous ways to experience the present through our senses. Although seeing,
touching, hearing, tasting and smelling can trigger memories from the past or future anticipations, these senses are
also very effective guides to the present, providing entrance
into the Big Circle.

You are probably the most aware of the fullness of a
sense experience when you see, touch, hear, taste or smell
something unique or special. How often have you mini-
mized one sense to enhance your experience of another?
You might close your eyes, for example, when listening to
beautiful music or when tasting your favorite food.

Challenge yourself to bring that same attention to
your everyday experiences. This exercise not only centers
you in the present moment, where all manifestation occurs, but it is also so enjoyable and informative that once

you get in the habit of entering the Big Circle in this way, you'll be eager to make it part of your daily Receive Practice.

exercise

Choose one of the senses and immerse yourself in that experience for sixty seconds. You can do it while waiting for the bus, in the grocery line or sitting at your desk at work.

Taste

Exercise: For sixty seconds, bring the same focus to a food from a typical meal that you give to a special-occasion food.

Result: By receiving all of the flavors of the food you eat every day, you will increase your appreciation for what you are eating. And you may discover, for example, that the lunch you pick up on the run lacks flavor or is too salty.

Sight

Exercise: For sixty seconds, bring the same attention to something you see on a typical day that you would give to an unusually beautiful sunset.

Result: By noticing what you look at every day, you will more fully appreciate what you see. And you may realize, for example, that you don't like the picture that has been hanging on your living room wall for the last twenty years.

Hearing

Exercise: For sixty seconds, bring the same concentration to a sound you hear on a typical day that you would give to your favorite music.

Result: Just as sound is used as a meditative device, as in repeating the word *OM*, the sounds you hear on a daily basis can bring relaxation. And you may become aware of background sounds from a television, for example, and decide it is noise you would like to eliminate.

(continued)

Touch

Exercise: For sixty seconds, bring the same attentiveness to something you handle or what or who touches you on a typical day that you would give to a new lover's caress or the softness of a favorite sweater.

Result: When you bring the same mindfulness to the objects you come into contact with every day, you will more fully appreciate the feel and textures of what you touch. And you may recognize, for example, that your pillow is as flat as a pancake and has been disturbing your sleep.

Smell

Exercise: For sixty seconds, bring the same awareness to a smell from a typical day that you would give to the fragrance of a bouquet of flowers.

Result: By paying attention to the smells you breathe in every day, you will more fully appreciate the scents in your everyday environment. And you may recall, for example, that you haven't cleaned your cat's litter box recently.

The Sixth Sense

Have you ever sensed that someone is looking at you and then turned around to find you are correct? When the phone rings, have you ever known who it is before you answer?

Intuitive flashes, strong hunches and psychic premonitions are all drawing from the Big Circle. This is the nonlocal space of which scientists speak. It is the area where psychics see pictures, hear words, smell smells or hold objects that they then interpret.

The five senses, when serving as conduits into the Big Circle, can lead us to the sixth sense. Many believe that we all have telepathic ability and that through practice we can strengthen our extrasensory gifts.

exercise

Throughout the day, bring your awareness to your senses. Choose one sense and spend sixty seconds in that sense experience. You can do it while waiting for the bus, in the grocery line or sitting at your desk at work.

stop chasing your tale!

My life has a superb cast but I can't figure out the plot.
—ASHLEIGH BRILLIANT

"After years of trying to find a partner, I finally gave up and accepted that I would be single. That's when I met him."

"My husband and I did every procedure available to conceive a baby. We finally started looking into adoption. That's when I became pregnant."

"Just when I gave up that we would find the perfect house for the perfect price and began looking at our second choices, we found our dream home."

These are not uncommon stories. Most of us know

somebody who had given up on a cherished dream only to discover it came to them. What is that mysterious force that delivers what is desired only when you stop trying to get it? On the face of it, it appears cruel. It seems like life is saying: *Don't want something too much!*

Sometimes we deal with this phenomenon by acting as if we don't want something in the secret hope that the pretended indifference will turn the magic key. Or if it looks possible that we will get a cherished goal, we knock on wood in the hope that the act will prevent our wish from running away.

What is the mechanism that grants our wishes sometimes and ignores them at other times? Throughout history, people have attempted to manifest their desires in many ways, including sacrificing animals and people to the gods or by conducting elaborate rituals.

We have modern-day versions of these such as: My wish will be granted if I do one or more of the following:

- I give money to charities.
- I attend church.
- I am helpful to my parents.
- I work overtime.
- I write affirmations.
- I forgive people who have wronged me.

- I increase my sense of self-worth.
- I promise I won't keep all of the money if I win the lottery.
- I feng shui my home.
- I create an altar.
- I meditate every day.

It's apparent that, just like our ancestors, we still don't have a clue about how to get what we want. Like a dog chases its tail, we end up chasing our own tales, doing again and again activities that don't yield results. If we do finally catch something, we are mystified by what exactly made it happen. Could the problem be that we are neither aware of nor interested in the needs or desires of others?

Imagine there is someone you very much want to date. You are crazy about this person and dream about him or her day and night. "How can I get this person?" you ask yourself.

The reality is if they don't want you, that's pretty much the end of the story. You won't get them to want you by doing the following:

- Giving money to charities
- Attending church

- Being helpful to your parents
- Working overtime
- Writing affirmations
- Forgiving people who have wronged you
- Increasing your sense of self-worth
- Promising to give away some of the money you win in the lottery
- Feng shui-ing your home
- Creating an altar
- Meditating every day

Our dreams and goals are often narcissistically oriented. It's as if another person's desires and needs don't count or even exist!

Now let's apply this idea to a work arena. If you want a job, but the people who are hiring don't want you, all of the above won't do anything to help you. The job has its own requirements and needs. And you may just not be the right match.

Our egos can feel bruised when the world doesn't grant us what we want. But we receive an important lesson about power: we don't control everything, no matter how wonderful our intentions or how strong our desires. So being really, really good and fabulously wonderful doesn't manifest our wishes; neither does focusing with laserlike intensity on the object of our desire.

When you set an intention, when you want something, it is important to listen to what your goals and people in them want from *you*. Life is a two-way street.

Receptivity is about being attentive and receiving not only your needs and desires, but also those of others. How will you ever know if you are a great match for someone or for your goal if you are chasing your tale, repeating what you want like a mantra, as if you were ordering something from a cafeteria? How will you ever know what or who wants *you*? The story we tell ourselves is often a monologue that leaves no opportunity for input.

Now, obviously we are manifesting and creating all of the time, whether or not we are happy with the results. The point is, when we are divided within ourselves, the Little Circle components have a lot of power, and they have their own agenda. The dueling strategies of the conscious and the subconscious tangle the energy.

Life speaks to you in myriad ways—through people, events, magazine articles and even TV commercials. All of the words in the Receptive States word list in chapter 1 are experiences of being receptive to how life communicates.

There are perfect matches for you, and when you are in

sync internally, with no Little Circle mavericks sabotaging you, your external world mirrors that beautiful harmony. It's like you have given yourself the right key to unlock the right door.

What tale are you chasing? That story is from a suffering past/fantasy future paradigm, which, as previously discussed, is a time line that is not designed to give what you desire.

Although our egos have an important function, they just don't have the bigger picture; they don't have an aerial view. They tell a tale with you as the star. But as compelling as that drama is, others have speaking roles, too. Strengthening your Receive Muscles helps you to hear what they are saying.

When chasing your dreams is not getting you what you want, review the Receptive States word list and spend time in those receptive states. Your goal speaks to you through them. Drop your suffering past/fantasy future story. Stop chasing your tale. You have a dream. Stand still, be still and let it catch up to you. And once it does—receive, thank and welcome it.

CHAPTER SIX

what stands between you and your goal?

Embracing Receiving

The Guest House

This being human is a guest house.
Every morning a new arrival.

A joy, a depression, a meanness,
some momentary awareness comes
as an unexpected visitor.

Welcome and entertain them all!
Even if they're a crowd of sorrows,

who violently sweep your house
empty of its furniture,
still, treat each guest honorably.
He may be clearing you out
for some new delight.

The dark thought, the shame, the malice,
meet them at the door laughing,
and invite them in.

Be grateful for whoever comes,
because each has been sent
*as a guide from beyond.**

—RUMI

the monster celebration

Imagine this: You are invited to a party that is held in your honor by someone who has hated you, talked behind your back, disrespected and devalued you. This person contacts you to say, "You are important to me. I am so sorry I have

*From *The Essential Rumi,* translated by Coleman Barks (New York: HarperCollins, 1995).

not included you in my life and have not been good to you. You mean the world to me. I love you. You are precious to me. I have changed, and if it takes the rest of my life, I will prove it to you. I dearly want your friendship. To make up for the way I have treated you and to let you know how sincere I am, I am starting by throwing you a fabulous party and I hope you will do me the great favor and honor of attending."

How would you react to such an invitation? With distrust, caution or cynicism? Or would you feel hopeful, curious and willing to give the relationship a chance?

When you create a Monster Celebration, you are inviting the parts of yourself that you have cast out into the Little Circle back into the Big Circle. Here is some of what you may have evicted: anger, hope, disappointment, laziness, vulnerability, competence, competitiveness, optimism.

How will this celebration help you manifest your goals? Disowned parts of the personality, or monsters in the closet, run everything from behind the scenes from below the threshold of your consciousness, from the Little Circle, from the closet. No *one* and no *thing* wants to be excluded, made unimportant or disrespected. If they are, they make themselves known to you in subversive ways. They make trouble.

When you want something such as to lose weight, to find a relationship, to get a job or to be healthy, these parts become energized and spring into action. They become the gatekeepers to your goal. Basically, you are not getting your goal until you include them, until you bring them into the Big Circle.

In the Monster Celebration exercise, we invite the "monsters" we have put in the closet to come out and join a party that we have created just for them. We want those parts that have been thrown out, tossed away, snubbed and devalued, to feel welcomed, included and celebrated.

I want you to think of these monsters as representatives of feelings—not real people. This is a task in using your imagination. I like to picture them as resembling the creatures from Maurice Sendak's illustrations from his children's book *Where the Wild Things Are.*

Before you create your own Monster Celebration, read through all of the exercises and the examples that follow from people who have experienced the Monster Celebration. One way to describe this work is "shadow work." As fun, interesting and revealing as this exercise is for many people, it is also very powerful.

CREATING A PARTY FOR YOUR MONSTER

You have a goal. Something is getting in the way of your manifesting it. Think about your goal and ask for one monster
that has something to do with preventing the manifestation
of your goal. You don't need to know who it is ahead of time.
The monster will make itself known to you in this exercise.

Let's begin. The following is a guided meditation that
helps you access your subconscious.

1. Make sure you are in a distraction-free environment. Get comfortable and close your eyes.
2. Create the setting for your party. Is it a formal
   affair or a beach party? Is it on the French Riv-
   iera or in your hometown? Is it catered? Have
   you hired musicians? Who is there? Have you
   invited only close friends or is it a huge gala with
   hundreds in attendance? Take your time and pay
   attention to the details. The reason for going
   to this effort is the same as the reason why you
   would want to have a fabulous party if you were
   inviting people near and dear to you. You would
   want them to have a great time and to feel welcome and comfortable.

Give these monsters that you have kept in the closet a reason to come out. You want them to feel important and to know that they are an addition to your life—a welcome one! You may even want your monster to be the guest of honor.

Since you are creating this party with your imagination, the sky's the limit! Spare no expense. Have fun with it.

3. Once the room is set up and your environment is just the way you want it, you are ready to receive your monster. You are, in fact, the "receiving line." Go to the closet and open the door. Invite only one monster to the party. That way, all of your attention is with only one, and your monster will feel extra important and special!

4. As the monster enters the room, welcome it! Let it know that you are delighted to have it come to the party. Then observe and see what happens. Stay with this part as long as it feels comfortable.

5. When the party is over, or if the monster is ready to go back into the closet earlier, begin to bring this exercise to an end. But before the monster

leaves, it may want to tell you something or ask
you a question.

6. Once the monster is back in the closet, come
   back to the present. Write down what occurred
   and any impressions you have.

Once you become familiar with your monster, it will
not need to go back into the closet nor will you want it to.
This is an organic process that takes time and is likely to require more than one visit. As you get to know your monster
over time and it experiences your interest and desire for a
relationship, the monster will transform—and so will you!

However, until that occurs, place it back into the closet.
Your monster represents something that you have kept hidden for a long time. And just like a person who has not been
included and socialized, its behaviors will be stunted, primal
and lack self-awareness. For example, if you have banished
anger to the closet, when you let it out it will make itself
known to you in your day-to-day life! This could occur in
a few different ways. You might feel an overwhelming rage,
you may meet this anger in a bully who tries to dominate
or degrade you, you may encounter people who are furious
with you and gang up on you. Respect your reasons for ban-
ishing this monster in the first place. It will take time and

care to get to know it. As your relationship with your monster develops, both you and your monster will transform. But this is not a quick process!

I will tell you a story from the early days of leading people through this exercise. I had eight people in one five-class Receive and Manifest tele-course, which takes place over the phone in a tele-conference. By the third class my students were excited by the changes that had occurred in their lives and were eager to learn the next step—the Monster Celebration.

After the Monster Celebration exercise, the participants relayed their experiences to our group. I discovered that many of them had not returned their monsters to their closets. I talked again about the advisability of this but, because time was short, I gave everybody a few final instructions to prepare the next class.

One week later, when we reconvened, I was surprised when I experienced the dark, depressing feeling in the class—which was very unusual! Quickly the participants began to complain about the process and became increasingly obstinate and unpleasant. It took me a while to realize what had happened—their monsters were acting out!

Lesson learned. Now I tell everybody, just as I am telling you, return your monster to the closet. You will reap many benefits by doing so. Also, your monster is given a chance to learn how to relate in a healthy manner.

This is the same reason why prisoners are taken to halfway houses once they are released. As a society, we recognize that you can't shut human beings away for a long time and then just throw them back unsupervised into society. Your monsters have been prisoners. And you have been their jailer.

I think I have belabored this point enough!

This is powerful work. Honor your process and take your time.

monster celebration examples

Martha's Monster
The Goal: A healthy, loving relationship
The Party: Buffet-style in one room
The Monster: A diva

When Martha, an overly accommodating person in her personal relationships, opened the closet door, she encountered a haughty diva monster that wouldn't even speak to her until she offered it food from the buffet.

Martha had expended little effort in creating a welcoming environment for her monster. Although she had been given carte blanche to create any party setting she wanted, she came up with a stark, bland room with only a buffet table—and not a very interesting one! I have found this lack of effort to be common. It shows that the subconscious is resisting the idea of honoring the monster.

Martha's relationship philosophy emphasized fairness and friendship. She bent over backward to be considerate to her partners—often to her own detriment. Her relationship history was to be attracted to people who did not treat her as thoughtfully as she treated them.

She was surprised when she saw a nose-up-in-the-air diva emerge from the closet. This was exactly the kind of person she despised! Yet it was this very monster that needed her acknowledgment. Martha's goal of meeting someone with whom she could experience a healthy, loving relationship needed this integration of arrogance and feelings of superiority—her inner diva.

As Martha got to know her diva through subsequent Monster Celebrations (with much more attention paid to her party environment), the monster and Martha became friends with a genuine appreciation for each other. Over time, the monster became less haughty and Martha became less judgmental of this showy figure.

Now that Martha was not "run" from behind the scenes by her attraction/repulsion to inconsiderate divas, she shed her overly accommodating nature and found herself drawn to considerate people and began to form healthy, loving relationships.

Sandy's Monster

The Goal: Ten people to sign up for her workshop
The Party: A casual beach party
The Monster: Mr. Mysterious

When only two people signed up for Sandy's workshop, she knew something was in the Little Circle and decided to investigate. She created a fun Monster Celebration beach party and was curious to see who would show up when she opened the closet door.

The monster that appeared was mysterious and clearly enjoyed the fact that no one could figure out who it was. As the monster circulated in the party, it caused curiosity among the participants, but since it did not reveal anything about itself, everyone quickly lost interest and the monster returned to the closet.

Sandy recognized the mystery monster as a part of herself that had been running her life from behind the scenes. Hiding was a safe posture for a little girl growing up who had been traumatized by the suicide of her mother and abuse from her father. This monster had appeared in many areas of her life, from being passed over for promotions at work because those in charge were unaware of her contributions, to marrying a man who was not fully committed to her—something she did not know at the time of her wedding—and who in many ways remained a mystery to her throughout the marriage.

The current manifestation of this mystery monster took the form of her omitting important information in the newspaper ads she had bought to advertise her workshop. She had neglected to include her contact information and the place where the workshop was to be held. Consequently, no one knew how to find her!

Sandy's mystery monster was impeding her goal by keeping her invisible, hard to reach and hard to know. To manifest her goal, she needed visibility.

Over time, through subsequent Monster Celebrations, Sandy got to know her mystery monster. These days, her bosses not only notice how hard she works but they have also promoted her. And she now includes contact information when she presents a workshop!

Donna's Monster

The Goal: Advancing in her profession
The Party: A glamorous uptown private party in
Manhattan
The Monster: A clingy, needy monster

In response to Donna's goal of advancing in her profession, she encountered a small, shy, clingy monster that leapt from the closet into her arms where it buried its head in her clothes and refused to look at anyone.

Donna has spent a lifetime feeling embarrassed by her vulnerability and neediness and did whatever she could to hide her shame. She came from a family background where strength and self-assurance were highly valued and any sign of vulnerability provided an invitation for emotional abuse. Yet it was this very monster that was preventing her from achieving the level of professional status she desired. Her neediness not only required her acknowledgment and compassion but it also needed to be celebrated.

Carrying her monster in her arms, Donna wandered around the swanky party, listening to a jazz trio, chatting with people and eating hors d'oeuvres that were offered by waiters in tuxedos.

Everybody at the party was interested in the monster, stopping to say hello and letting it know how happy they were that the monster had attended. After a while Donna could feel the monster relax as it peered out at the people, the food and the musicians.

By the end of the party, the monster was sitting happily on a couch surrounded by partygoers. When Donna retrieved her monster from its admirers and walked it back to the closet door, they hugged each other. Donna told her monster how happy she was that it had enjoyed the party and promised to include it in her plans and in her life more often.

Over time, Donna grew more comfortable including her shy, clingy monster, and as a result her professional life blossomed.

Jack's Monster
The Goal: New friends
The Party: A neighborhood softball game
The Monster: A glass-is-always-half-full Pollyanna

We don't disown only the difficult parts of our personalities. Jack was surprised to find that one of his monsters was exceedingly cheerful.

Living in a large city, Jack had difficulty meeting new people. Although his social life was important to him, he had trouble making friends.

Jack decided to create an outdoor party in a park close to where he lived. A softball game seemed to offer a great way to meet new people.

Jack was surprised to see an overly friendly, optimistic monster emerge from the closet. As the game commenced with the happy monster eagerly waiting for its turn at bat, Jack realized that he overvalued his cynical personality components and had disowned this joyful, expressive part of himself.

Because our monsters in the closet have been there for a long time, they are not used to being out in the open and around people. Therefore their behavior and the way they relate is often a bit off. Although Jack's monster was cheerful, its behavior was over-the-top Pollyanna behavior.

As Jack continued to bring this monster to group events, his own behavior became more friendly and outgoing which in turn, helped him make new friends. And over time, his monster also began to relax and relate more appropriately.

Terry's Monster

The Goal: Her own private law practice
The Party: An expensive, elaborate high-society
party in her city's best hotel
The Monster: A small, emaciated monster

When Terry opened the closet door, a small, emaciated monster was unable to pay attention to anything she said because it was hungry. In fact, the entire time she was trying to engage the monster in conversation, it was stuffing its mouth with food it retrieved from the kitchen!

She decided to stop talking and help by giving it food so it would not have to keep going to the kitchen. Although no conversation was possible in that first Monster Celebration encounter, Terry, an overachiever, realized that she had "starved" a part of her personality that desperately needed nourishment. It took several more Monster Celebration exercises before her monster had eaten enough food to participate in a conversation.

Terry's goal was to leave her secure government job where she worked as an attorney and start her own law practice. She came from a family where her parents and most family members were employed by the government in civil service jobs. They had spent their working lives with job security and ultimately a generous pension.

As much as Terry wanted her own law practice, the truth was she was ambivalent about what an independent self-employed life would offer. She was afraid she would not be able to financially take care of herself— something that this high-achieving woman did not like to acknowledge—and had consequently starved a monster that needed recognition.

As Terry continued to cultivate private clients, she also invested in her relationship with this monster. Over time, not only did they become friends but she also increasingly gained clients while the monster gained weight. She eventually turned a room in her house into a home office. And keeping a tradition started at the first Monster Celebration, she always made sure she sent her monster back to the closet with a doggie bag filled with food.

Sam's Monster
The Goal: Three new clients
The Party: An empty room
The Monster: A loudmouthed show-off

Sam, a businessman, was worried about losing his job— work that required cultivating clients for his company. Unable to secure the three clients on whom he had set his sights, he created a Monster Celebration to find out what monster was preventing him from reaching his goal.

It is noteworthy that for this Monster Celebration, he barely bothered to set up the environment for his party. In fact, as it turned out, he had a lot of resentment about creating a celebration at all.

The monster that came out of the closet was loud-mouthed and acted as if it was the greatest monster of all! He swaggered when he walked and referred to himself as a "monsta," the way someone would use the word *gangsta* instead of *gangster*.

Sam felt embarrassed by this monster and wanted nothing to do with him at the Monster Celebration party. When he described him to me, I was reminded of how teenagers, as they are trying on different identities, exhibit just this kind of strut and swagger. I asked him if he was ever made fun of when he was a teenager.

He described feeling humiliated by his parents whenever he stepped out of the role into which he had been cast. Being "too big for his britches" got him laughed at and put down.

This monster's behavior was not only reminiscent of what caused Sam embarrassment in his youth, but these qualities also provoked the same revulsion in him as an adult. When he encountered people who had the characteristics mirrored by the monster, he not only judged them he also tried to get away from them.

Yet, this is the monster that most needed his love and acceptance and it wanted to get into the Big Circle. This was the monster that was preventing him from reaching his goal.

I asked Sam if he was behaving in a way that he thought a businessman was supposed to behave, rather than being his authentic self. I learned that he was not only trying on the persona of a successful businessman, which was not helping him, but also the tension resulting from this was draining him of energy and hope.

I asked him to create a new Monster Celebration, this time one that was welcoming. Although Sam continued to have substantial resistance to constructing a party for a monster that had caused him so much grief throughout his life, he was committed to this process and created a more welcoming party. He reinvited his "monsta." This time he managed to be friendlier, and the monster responded to his effort.

Although Sam was going to have to spend more time with this monster to form a good relationship, even after just two Monster Celebrations, he was able to sign up two of the three clients he had set as his goal. The third one—a loudmouthed show-off, it so happens—was still uncommitted but Sam felt confident, due to his new insight, that he would be able to bring him into the company also.

Inviting this monster to the party and into the Big Circle offered Sam the opportunity to be aware of this figure when it showed up in his life. His challenge, shared by everyone who embarks on the journey of monster integration, was this: Would he be able to be as considerate when he met this "monsta" in his daily life? Would he be able to have compassion and understanding for this person? And would Sam be easy on himself when he spotted the "monsta" within?

Nancy's Monsters

The Goal: Double her monthly income
The Party: An empty room followed by a big,
expensive party
The Monsters: The Blamer, the Isolator,
the Controller and the Rebel

How do monsters prevent goals from manifesting? Below is a story about a participant in one of my Receive and Manifest courses who ultimately refused to accept and embrace her monsters. I am using this example because her resistance represents the sheer power of a Little Circle inhabitant's ability to sabotage goals. Even though I instructed the class to bring out only one monster, Nancy brought out several.

Nancy's goal was to double her monthly income by the end of the five-week course. During the Monster Celebration, she met her monsters: the Blamer, the Isolator, the Controller and the Rebel. These monsters were the gate-keepers to her goal, as are all monsters. They were also the money that she wanted to double. Let me explain.

Nancy complained that a lack of money was the source of her problems. She *blamed* her life conditions on not having more money, she *isolated* herself because she didn't have enough money to go out, she felt *controlled* by not having more money and she was *rebellious* as a habitual response to suggestions about how to improve her financial circumstances. Do you see that the goal of doubling her income and her monsters were one and the same? It was as if money itself was in the closet.

These monsters want to come into the Big Circle, to be received and embraced. They are what stand between Nancy and her goal. At the same time, they are the goal itself.

In the Big Circle, *nothing* is separate. It is *we* who have banished the Little Circle inhabitants because we are uncomfortable with them. Yet they want to be included in the

Big Circle, to come to the party or, to paraphrase Cinderella, they "want to go to the ball!"

In her first Monster Celebration party, Nancy's monsters refused to come out of the closet. I don't blame them! She had not bothered to set up a welcoming festive environment. In fact, the room was empty.

At my urging, Nancy created a new Monster Celebration. This time she went in the opposite direction and constructed a very big, expensive party for her monsters. Notice that a woman who had a poor relationship with money was spending a great deal of it for the celebration! In fact, this time she decided to ask her monsters what kind of party they would enjoy. Although the monsters were not the most gregarious bunch when they arrived, they did seem to have a good time.

When Nancy first reported back to our class, she was excited by the possibility that her Monster Celebration would help manifest her goal of doubling her income. Her excitement, however, was short-lived.

Even though, within a day of her Celebration, a friend offered her part-time work, which would have helped her with her goal, instead of feeling grateful, she reverted to her previously cynical, unpleasant attitude and complained to the class about the futility of the exercise.

I have an image of a group of dollar bills and money of other denominations sitting in her closet playing poker: rebel bill, control bill, isolation bill and blame bill. This is the money that Nancy wanted to come to her.

Her inability to show any appreciation for the offer of part-time work, or appreciation for the exercise and ultimately the course itself, served to keep her in the very same financial condition that her goal was to improve.

YOUR MONSTER CELEBRATION

Think of your own goal. Give your monsters a reason to come out of the closet. Embracing, celebrating and getting to know your monsters softens them, makes them less shy, less freaked out, less mean, more honest, happier, more relaxed, less isolated, more connected, less guarded, less distracted, more considerate, less lonely, less argumentative and less fearful (it is *you* that they are afraid of!). The party welcomes them back into the fold (the Big Circle), which is just where you want them to be so they can help you rather than obstruct you.

CHAPTER SEVEN

love your goal and it will love you back

*Bringing Receiving and
Giving into Balance*

It's human nature to like people who like you. People get jobs because the interviewer likes them. Personal relationships are formed when two people like each other. Children are happier when they feel loved and liked by their parents. Your goal wants to be liked and loved, too.

How do you feel about your goal? Be honest. Are you ambivalent? Do you treat your goal disrespectfully? Or do you love your goal?

If you want a new car, ask yourself: How do I treat the one I have?

If you want to lose weight, ask yourself: How do I
    treat my food?
If you want a relationship, ask yourself: How do I
    treat the people I see every day?
If you want better health, ask yourself: How do I
    treat my body?
If you want a better job, ask yourself: How do I
    treat the one I have?

In the following pages, you will read about people who formed loving relationships with their goals. Keep in mind as you read about them that each of these people kept a gratitude journal, had committed to a Complaint Fast and participated in the Receive Exercises described previously in this book.

receiving money

If your goal is to have more money and you talk about the unimportance of money, why would your goal want to come near you? If you think it's unspiritual to want money, it will find someone else who has a better opinion of it. If you talk about being broke all the time, the money you have won't feel appreciated—and unappreciated money won't multiply. The following example shows how a gifted massage therapist chases away money.

"I don't do this for the money," my massage therapist Molly said. As I sat on her living room couch waiting for her prior client to leave—a woman who spent an inordinate amount of time rifling through her purse before announcing that she had neglected to bring a checkbook or cash with her to the appointment.

"Not a problem," Molly exclaimed brightly. "Just send it whenever you can or bring it with you next time you come."

As I enjoyed the gentle touch of her hands massaging my muscles, I noted that this was the same woman who complained incessantly about her money problems. Yet she told her client that her inability to pay was unimportant.

While undercharging for services is epidemic in the helping fields, Molly charged even less than most people in her profession. Believing it is incongruous to be helpful to people and to be paid for it can easily pave the road to financial difficulty.

If you are not a skilled Receiver, you may have trouble asking for a raise, requesting a living wage, determining the value of your services or skills, or lending money you never get back. Your ideas about money can easily prevent it from coming your way.

Here are two exercises that are versions of Receive Exercises that I have previously outlined:

Money-Attracting Exercises

Place money of different denominations around your house or apartment. For example, put a dollar bill on your kitchen table, a ten-dollar bill on the TV and a quarter on your couch. Every time you pass by them, say something complimentary like, "You look so beautiful today!" or, "You are amazing! I love you so much!" Fuss over them. Coo over them. Show them how glad you are that they are with you!

Organize the money in your wallet. You may want to have your paper money face in the same direction or group your one-dollar bills together, your five-dollar bills together, etc. The point of this exercise is to pay positive attention to the money you currently have in your possession. Don't shove crumpled money into your purse or have pennies and dimes scattered all over the place. Would you want to hang around someone who treated you that way?

DIANE'S STORY

An astrologer with a private practice, Diane wanted to increase her income by attracting more clients. Within days of writing down her goal, she was contacted by several people requesting appointments, although most of them wanted to barter or asked if she would reduce her fee.

Diane was not discouraged by this response. She was pleased with her progress. Increasing her receptivity through her Receive Exercises had attracted interest in her services. However, she realized that due to her history of bartering, she seemed to be a magnet for people who had little or no money to pay for them.

Just like a person, your goal doesn't automatically incorporate new information that you have not thought much about, let alone communicated. It took this experience for Diane to become conscious about her desire to break from past business practices. Earlier in her career, bartering had been a helpful way for her to introduce people to her services. But that time was long gone and she realized that she had not kept current with where she was presently in her career. She was ready for a new business plan.

Diane rewrote her goal to include the word *paying* before *clients*. Once she was specific, her goal knew what to deliver.

CHUCK'S STORY

Chuck's goal was to receive $1,000 extra in his paycheck each month in anticipation of his upcoming retirement. He wanted to travel and knew this would require additional funds. Chuck wrote down his goal, and two days later his boss informed him that the company's retirement plan was being revamped and an extra $1,000 would be included each month in his pension check.

Chuck's goal manifested quickly because he and his goal were not in conflict. He was comfortable stating it and writing it. Although his goal didn't manifest exactly the way he thought it would—he thought the increase would be in his salary—because he had clear communication with his goal and there weren't Little Circle components undermining his wish, he was able to materialize his goal quickly.

receiving work

Work that is satisfying, energizing and makes full use of one's talents is an elusive dream for many. You may know what you want to do for work, but don't know how to manifest it. You may be unable to even imagine a rewarding work life.

When a job is your goal, the first step is to have some idea of what you would like to do so you can clearly communicate it to your goal. If you don't know, the Send Cinderella to Rehab exercise discussed in chapter 3 will help clear out the debris that is preventing ideas from coming through to you.

If you know what job you want but haven't been able to manifest it, write it down in one concise sentence so that your goal knows you are ready to receive the job. Once you have written it down, your goal will begin to speak to you. It is your task to be an open Receiver, so you can "hear" what your goal has to say.

Whether you want to advance in the company for which you presently work or you are looking for a new job, think of your goal as evaluating your qualifications and wondering whether or not you would be an asset to the desired job. Your goal will maintain interest in you in ratio to your job attractiveness. So your first job is to become attractive to your goal.

Here are two exercises that are versions of Receive Exercises that I have previously outlined.

Work-Attracting Exercises

Are you a good personality fit for your job choice? Do you have the right temperament? How do people receive you? Spend several days noticing, observing, listening, accepting (notice these are words from the Receptive States word list) how people respond to you. If your goal is to advance in your company or if you are presently employed, apply this exercise to the people in your work environment. If you don't have a job, apply this to everyone with whom you are in contact. Once you receive the above information, analyze (an experience from the Active States word list) whether you need to make changes or adjustments or look for a different job.

Work life is one of the topics that people complain about the most. This has got to stop! Commit to your Complaint Fast. (Remember complaining is not the same as talking about your feelings.) Write a list of five wonderful attributes of the work you have or the job you want. Add to your list each day. When you commit to this exercise—both the Complaint Fast and the list—you are not denying negative or uncomfortable feelings. You are putting your best foot forward. Your goal will notice.

ROBERT'S STORY

Robert worked a day job he didn't like and that made him little money. He had been trying to develop a hypnotherapy practice, with limited success. When he enrolled in my course, he was scheduling only one or two clients a month. His goal was to increase the number of clients. Since he wanted 150 clients over the next year, he made this number manageable by breaking it down to a goal of gaining five clients a week.

A person who applied himself diligently to his Receive Exercises, Robert achieved early success. In the first week he booked five sessions although only three of the people kept their appointments. The following week, he secured three more bookings, and all of the clients showed up. However, since he didn't reach his goal of five clients, he created a Monster Celebration to get to know the Little Circle inhabitants who were preventing clients from contacting him.

He discovered two monsters: one was super-responsible and the other was judgmental about receiving money for services designed to help people. Robert wanted to bring these monsters into the Big Circle.

He began by doing the Send Cinderella to Rehab exercise, writing in his journal about all of the money, objects and lifestyles he desired. Next, he acknowledged his negative view of responsibility and his judgment about the way money should be earned and breathed them in and out. He included these monsters in his day-to-day awareness; he wrote in his journal about them and dialogued with them. He knew he and his monsters needed to become allies.

The deepening of these monster friendships opened the metaphorical door as he began to welcome clients with money conflicts and those learning about the benefits of responsibility. In this way, he not only included his own monsters in the Big Circle, but he also included other people's monsters as well.

CAROLYN'S STORY

Carolyn didn't expect to lose her job as the result of her goal: *Receive the benefits of the work that I have done for the last six years and focus more on my personal life.*

A human resources director for a large company, Carolyn felt overworked and unappreciated. She had little time to spend with her recently retired husband and wanted a job that required fewer hours. Most important, she wanted to feel valued by her coworkers.

During a long-planned vacation, she and her husband met a couple. The wife's career as a life coach fascinated Carolyn. The more she heard about it, the more she related her own skills as being a match for this type of work. After she returned home, she not only began to research what it would take to be a life coach but she also began to look into other interesting work possibilities. Then she was laid off.

Carolyn relayed to her classmates that prior to the Receive and Manifest course, she would have experienced this turn of events as a tragedy instead of as a conversation with her goal.

A comfortable severance package freed her to pursue other lines of work. She answered an ad for a human resources director. She had kept a real estate license current through the years and considered becoming a real estate agent. "Receive everything—decide later," she thought. "I want to stay open to all of the possibilities."

Carolyn was gratified and touched by the response of her coworkers to her being laid off. As they expressed their condolences and said how much she would be missed, she experienced for the first time how highly regarded she was and how fondly people thought of her.

After taking the time to explore a variety of options, she eventually decided to pursue work in real estate. She felt that returning to this work would give her the opportunity to spend more time with her husband and that her love of working with people would be a perfect match for this job.

"These days I sit out on my deck with my husband, drinking my morning coffee. I am so much happier. I am relaxed and am grateful for each day. And I still run into people with whom I used to work, and they say it just isn't the same without me!"

receiving relationships

The relationship with your goal mirrors the relationships you have with others, and nowhere is this more evident than in your intimate relationships.

Not long ago, I watched young women on a TV show talking about how reticent they were about opening their hearts to love. Teary-eyed, they explained that they had been hurt in previous relationships. They were twenty-three years old!

Who among us has not talked about a bad relationship, a painful break-up or a betrayal? It takes strength to open your heart and emotions to receive love! You are challenged to remain in the present with a current individual, rather than retreating to the suffering past/fantasy future time line.

You will chase away a potential partner if you talk about your suffering past or your vision for your fantasy future. Your goal wants to deliver a fabulous partner. Help your goal help you.

Here are two exercises that are versions of Receive Exercises that I have previously outlined.

Relationship-Attracting Exercises

Communicate clearly. When you let your goal know what you want by writing it down, you are also being clear to yourself about what you desire. Too often, people's wish for a mate lacks specificity. If someone asks you for the top five qualities you want in a relationship partner, do you have to think about it? Or do you know? Tell your goal exactly what you want.

Honesty is essential. Receiving a relationship requires first receiving where you are right here, right now—not where you don't want to be or where you wish you were— which is, of course the suffering past and fantasy future. Manifestation occurs in the present, in the Big Circle. Ask yourself the following questions.

- Do you have monsters in the closet that are getting in the way and need to be welcomed into the Big Circle?
- Are you high maintenance, requiring your goal to jump through multiple hoops to get to you?
- Do you complain (aloud or silently) about re-

lationships or about the people you have been with in the past? (Remember this is not the same as expressing your feelings.)

- Are you sincerely grateful for the people who are currently in your life?
- Are you looking for a mate to rescue you or to happily bond with the person you are today?
- Do you incorporate, value and exhibit the traits in yourself that you seek in another?

TANYA'S STORY

Tanya's goal was to travel with her boyfriend. She wrote: *I want to accompany my boyfriend on his international business travels.*

At the time Tanya enrolled in my course, she was dating a businessman who traveled frequently as a requirement of his work and she wanted to spend more time with him. Within a month of writing her goal, Tanya's relationship ended, leaving her heartbroken.

As she breathed *heartbreak* in . . . and out, she was convinced her goal had abandoned her. The magnetic pull to enter her suffering past and fantasy future was strong, though she resisted it as often as she could by utilizing the breathing exercise to stay in the present.

As the days became weeks, her understanding of this relationship deepened and she was able to accept that it was for the best that it had ended. By the time she went to her brother-in-law's company Christmas party that year, she was open to meeting someone.

The day after the party, she received a phone call from a man she had met the previous night. He asked her for a date. She liked him and welcomed the invitation.

He turned out to be the mate she had yearned for, and soon she was *accompanying her boyfriend on his international business travels.* The only difference was that he was not the man she thought she would be accompanying! Over time the relationship blossomed and they ultimately married.

JENNIFER'S STORY

Jennifer had a long history of being attracted to men who didn't want to commit to her. Receiving the reality that she was in love with and had invested in a four-year relationship with a man who was not willing to marry her (something she very much wanted) was painful. She was determined to change her pattern and meet a suitable relationship partner.

With this in mind, Jennifer was very specific when she

wrote her goal. She wanted her goal to be clear about what she wanted and that required that she communicate clearly. Otherwise her goal would not realize how much she had changed. Here is what Jennifer wrote: *I want to attract a marriage-minded, emotionally healthy, intelligent and fun, kind and loving man.*

As her heart began the journey of healing, Jennifer's goal began to communicate to her. She e-mailed the following message to her classmates:

> *Thought I would share a fun experience. When I was in San Francisco last week, I had an Asian-style lunch. Dessert was a fortune cookie. The fortune read: "Be prepared to receive something special." I thought this was a fun message from the universe letting me know that I'm on track.*

Next, Jennifer created a Monster Celebration. After setting up the party, she opened the closet door and a stack of little monsters standing on each others' shoulders gracefully fell in succession to the floor and then did a backwards domino effect, so that the last monster was pushed forward facing her. She said hello to the one in front who was "orange, friendly and cute," and asked who he was. "You," he said. When she asked which part of Jennifer he was, he responded, "I am all of you."

"What am I afraid of?"

"Of love," he said. "You are fearful of being loved. You have all of this love to give and yet you are afraid to receive it."

When they hugged, he turned from orange to a beautiful pinkish red. He walked back to the closet, opened the door and winked at her before closing the door behind him.

Jennifer's monster brilliantly demonstrated the "domino" effect that occurs for so many. Painful experiences from past relationships accumulate and are relegated to the Little Circle where they become monsters in the closet. Jennifer had been unaware of how much she was submerging her feelings about the past.

She told our class, "That was a powerful and a highly emotional experience for me. Who knew all of this stuff was in there! What a freeing experience."

A month later, Jennifer reported, "I wanted to share with everyone that my receiving continues every single day, and I am in a new relationship with a wonderful man."

The next month, she wrote: "The relationship is going very well. He is exactly what I asked for: marriage-minded, emotionally healthy, kind, intelligent, fun, loving and so much more. The gift of receiving is truly amazing. I've changed up my goal a bit now to reflect the following (I still write in my Receive Journal every single day!): I am grateful for being in a marriage-minded, long-term, loving relationship."

Although Jennifer did not end up marrying him, they parted friends. It was a year later that she met her future husband.

receiving health

Disregard your feelings, and you pay an emotional price. Pay no attention to what you think, and you inhibit mental ease. But it's your physical body that you use to get out of bed, get to work or cook dinner. And if your body tells you something and you don't listen, you are likely to pay a physical price.

Research has long suggested that the mind, emotions and body are connected. Consider the following links between health and receiving and how our bodies speak to us and for us:

- A closed heart doesn't *receive* love.
- Closed arteries prevent the heart from *receiving* blood.

- Smoky lungs can't *receive* air.
- Clogged pores prevent the skin from *receiving* nourishment.
- A closed mind can't *receive* information.
- Arms crossed broadcast the message "Don't come near me. I won't *receive* you."
- A closed expression says, "I'm not *receiving* you."
- We close our eyes when we don't want to *receive* something visually.
- We close our ears when we don't want to *receive* an auditory message.

It's easy to become angry with your body when it is not cooperating. Yet, when you don't feel well, what your body needs more than anything is your compassion. Anger sets up an adversarial relationship that produces stress, tension and exhaustion—none of which are helpful for your healing.

Here are two exercises that are versions of Receive Exercises that I have previously outlined.

Health-Attracting Exercises

To help you attract good health, review the Receptive States word list (in chapter 1) and spend time in those receptive states while you adjust your relationship with your body. You may want to carry a copy of this word list with you as a reminder to strengthen your receptivity each day.

- *Observe* your body. What is it showing you?
- *Listen to* your body. What is it telling you?
- *Appreciate* your body. How does your body respond to your appreciation?
- *Notice* your body. How does your body feel about being on your radar screen?
- *Relax* your body. How does your body respond?

Invest in a healthy, open dialogue. Tell your body what you want. And then receive. Your body will communicate and let you know what feels comfortable. All healthy relationships take into account both participants. Neither a person nor a body wants to be treated inconsiderately. An appreciated, acknowledged body is happy.

CATHY'S STORY

Cathy suffered from chronic fatigue. And although her primary goal was to have a child, she wanted to be strong and healthy before she attempted to conceive. She wrote her goal: *I want to restore my good health so I can have a child.*

An overachiever by her own definition, Cathy was highly disciplined and allowed herself little downtime. But, over time, she began to pay a high price. Her body began to rebel, first with kidney stones, and then with deteriorating energy reserves.

Angry with her body for "letting her down," as she thought of it, Cathy continued her high-energy lifestyle and was eventually diagnosed with the immune disorder chronic fatigue syndrome. She refused to accept this diagnosis, and as she extended well past her energy reserves, the resulting physical depletion boomeranged back into her mental and emotional state.

When Cathy enrolled in my Receive and Manifest course, she was eager to regain her good health. As it is for many people, the concept that receiving is helpful was new to her, and she initially had trouble understanding its value.

Her breakthrough occurred when she created a Monster Celebration and invited a monster that was inhibiting her goal to become healthy. Her party was a just-for-girls slumber party where the girls played with makeup, tried on shoes and ate popcorn. (Notice how childlike and playful this scene is for an overachiever!)

When she opened the closet door, a big fuzzy "grandfatherly" figure appeared, exuding the qualities of *acceptance*, *reassurance* and *graciousness*. He sat down with the girls and watched, smiled and enjoyed the party.

After the exercise, Cathy exclaimed, "Acceptance is so hard for me! I never accept! In fact, at my wedding, the best man said during his toast about me: 'Cathy is always trying to do better, to improve herself.' I've always felt so proud about that part of me."

To Cathy, *acceptance* meant *passivity*. It meant settling for what she didn't want and somehow having to make it okay. In fact, *not* accepting her illness kept her hope alive that she might someday overcome it.

If Cathy *accepted* her illness, *reassured* herself that she could heal and was *gracious* (courteous) to her body, she would give herself the opportunity to respond to her physical condition in the present time, and that, in turn, would help her heal.

Reframing *acceptance* as acknowledging what is here right now helped Cathy to change how she thought about her illness. Once she knew that she wasn't giving up and resigning herself to poor health, she was easier on herself, which in turn led her to explore possibilities for healing.

I love the way Cathy directed her achievement-oriented

personality. Throughout the five-week course, even when she was not totally convinced of their value, she embraced the Receive concepts and diligently completed each exercise. She recorded her daily gratitudes and began graciously accepting compliments. She became self-revealing and told people about her condition. She stopped feeling ashamed about her poor health and brought her chronic fatigue into the Big Circle. She also became aware of how some of her friends and activities were draining instead of energizing her and she made changes in how and with whom she spent her time.

"I am less stressed and my boundaries are clearer and firmer," she reported to her classmates.

Over the following two years, Cathy strengthened her Receive Practice and her health steadily improved. As a result, she was ready to become a mother, and months after her decision Cathy gave birth to a beautiful baby girl.

JONATHAN'S STORY

Jonathan entered my five-week course with nearly total hearing loss in his left ear. This condition had begun two months prior, and he naturally had a goal of regaining his hearing.

After the first class, Jonathan made a connection between listening and hearing loss. "I've spent my life hearing but not listening," he said. "I am going to change that and come to each class prepared to listen."

Jonathan's transformation was evident. He did the Receive Exercises faithfully and reported each week that his hearing was improving.

His Monster Celebration party was poignant in that he was unable to create a party atmosphere. A somber and intense man, Jonathan concluded that having had no experience with celebration or joy in his life, he didn't know how to create a party. He decided to bring *celebration* and *joy* into the Big Circle.

Although he regained sixty percent of his hearing just prior to the fifth and last class, Jonathan's doctor informed him that an operation would still be necessary to equalize the pressure in his ear. Dreading the operation, he was grateful when, during the night before the last class, his ear pressure equalized, which made surgery unnecessary.

receiving food

Thank you for this food we are about to eat. Many of us grew up with families who began each meal with a blessing. These prayers followed people from generation to generation like an affectionate family member showing up when everyone sat down at the dinner table.

These days, this honoring ritual is largely absent as we pick up food in a bag at a drive-through window, eat from cartons taken directly from the refrigerator without bothering to put the food on a plate or sit down, and spend meal times separated from family members.

It's easy to understand why food may feel neglected! Mistreated, unacknowledged food hangs out in the Little Circle running you from behind the scenes like a recalcitrant child. It tugs at you when you have other things to do and makes demands that you pay attention to it when you would much rather think of something else.

Just as in all of the other parts of your life that I've discussed up until now, your food is appreciative when you relate to it in a thoughtful, loving, respectful manner. The following exercises are versions of Receive Exercises previously outlined.

Weight-Loss-Attracting Exercises

Count your blessings

- Honor your food and express your gratitude.
- Write in your gratitude journal how grateful you are for your food.

Be aware of your senses

- When you eat your food, experience your five senses to enter the present moment and the Big Circle.
- Notice what is on your plate, chew slowly, appreciate the flavors and experience the textures.

Appreciate your food

- Don't treat everyday food as boring and unimportant. Give it the same gratitude, interest and excitement that you offer a favorite meal.
- Be respectful! Appreciated food is more likely to deliver all of its nutrients.

Commit to a Complaint Fast

* Don't complain about your food.

Feel your feelings

* Don't require your food to be a workhorse for your emotions. It wasn't designed for that job.
* Nurture and nourish your feelings, rather than making the food an unappreciated stand-in.

Be self-revealing

* Talk to your food. Let it speak to you, too. Create a deep, authentic relationship.
* Don't have a hit-and-run or drive-by relationship. It will feel like a cheap date!
* Write a letter to your food.

Breathe in . . . and out . . .

* Breathe in and out the emotions you are asking the food to handle.
* Don't be frightened of feeling bored, lonely or

sad. Those feelings are part of the human experience. Bring them into the Big Circle, where they can hang out with all of your other feelings.

Don't recite a story of your suffering past and fantasy future

- Don't complain to yourself or others that you have *always* had a hard time losing weight and you hope you will *never* have that experience again.

Receive everything—decide later

- Don't buy into the idea that if you love food, you'll never stop eating it. That would be the same as thinking, *If I listen to you, I'll have to do what you say or I'll never get my turn to speak.*

Love your food

- And it will love you, too.

CAROL'S STORY

Carol had been dieting on and off since she was a young woman. Now in her early fifties, and having successfully manifested her dream job, she had the confidence to make weight loss her goal.

First she wanted to get her goal's attention, so she wrote in her Receive Journal: *I will be fit, lighter, and healthier in three months, releasing ten pounds per month and increasing my activities.* Carol did not agonize about how to write the goal since she was an advanced Receiver. She knew the goal might change once the dialogue began, once the relationship was formed.

Already in the habit of writing her gratitudes each day in her Receive Journal and doing the sixty-second visualization, she made a point to begin including gratitudes related to food.

She considered potatoes her archenemy, so her first task was to bring potatoes out of the Little Circle and into the Big Circle. She needed a good relationship with potatoes so they would not run her from behind the scenes, showing up as cravings and obsessions.

She bought a Mr. Potato Head toy to place on her kitchen counter. As soon as she decided to create a positive relationship with potatoes, they began to show up everywhere. She saw articles about potatoes and people began bringing them up in conversation. When she visited a local nursery to buy plants, the sales person told her they had potato vines, which she promptly bought. Her boyfriend, who did not know about this project, began talking about the potato famine in Ireland!

All of this did not make her want to eat more potatoes. It had the opposite effect—she was no longer obsessing about them.

She began to eat healthier food, which she equated to bringing all foods into the Big Circle. "Since all the foods are there, I make better choices," she reported.

She also remarked, "I had a marvelous meal at a restaurant on Sunday. Inviting restaurant experiences in as a normal activity seemed to take away the *I get to eat whatever I want since I am at a restaurant* feeling." She went on to tell me about the friend with whom she had dined, "My friend asks herself twice if she wants something every time she eats. She is a total lover of food, is in great shape and has the best relationship with food of anyone I know. We are planning on meeting up in Ireland, and I asked her about places she would like to go. Her answer was: *My priorities are scenery and food.*"

Within a short time after writing her goal, Carol began attending a gym. (Conveniently, her workplace had gym facilities on-site.) And, as she gained confidence, she decided to write a letter to her food.

After a month had passed, she revised her goal to: *My*

goal is to create a fabulous, supportive and loving relationship with food. Carol had significantly changed her relationship with food. She was making healthier choices and had increased her activities, but she had lost only three of the planned ten pounds.

She decided to get additional support and joined Weight Watchers. She recorded her progress in a notebook. Comfortable with her new goal, she was open to the continuing dialogue. Her goal's next message came in an unexpected way.

One day, as she and her boyfriend were out for a two-hour walk, something they did frequently now, he said in the middle of a heated conversation, "You don't have room for discord in a relationship." She recognized the truth of his statement and decided to investigate further.

She set up a party for a Monster Celebration and invited a monster that related to this issue of discord and her conflicts with food. Who was in the Little Circle? Who wanted to get into the Big Circle?

When she opened the closet door, a four-foot pointy-headed, loud-mouthed critic emerged. Among the criticisms that he immediately hurled at her was this statement: "You're lazy, inconsistent and not working hard enough!"

Carol's first response was to ignore the insults as she

pasted on a "hostess smile." The exasperated critic said: "You're not listening to me." He shrunk and then dissolved.

Ignoring, deflecting and not listening or responding was her common reaction to criticism. She spent her childhood closing her ears to the discord and sniping that raged between her parents and toward her.

It's a great safety mechanism for a child, and it made sense to Carol that she had placed criticism, feedback and unsolicited advice in the Little Circle. But what could its value be to her now? Her four-foot critic was not nice to her. She felt vulnerable.

Carol decided to "Receive everything—decide later" and returned to the closet to re-invite her critic to the party. This time, she was determined to listen and reserve judgment.

In response to Carol's new approach, her critic was less critical, while remaining serious and pointed in what he had to say. He had plenty of advice for how she could help herself. Carol listened to everything, which was a big step.

"I'll think about what you've said," she told her critic.

As she reflected later on the experience, she realized that her critic was essentially an expert—an expert on *her*. She had a lot to think about and wasn't sure yet what the impact of opening this dialogue would be.

Over time, Carol began to relax. She brought criticism

into the Big Circle and discovered that listening was helpful to her, that it had value.

Creating a long-term, healthy relationship with food was a process, as it is for many who have had a history of not trusting food. Carol continues to lose weight in ratio to her ability to maintain a healthy relationship with food. She still finds herself, from time to time, repeating her lifetime habit of treating food poorly, but she discovers that each time she is respectful and loving toward her food, the food responds in kind by being helpful and loving to her.

strengthening your relationship with all of your goals

Your Ongoing Receive Practice

the butterfly effect

A dream strongly desired creates a ripple effect. And life responds. There is a saying that describes this interconnectedness: A butterfly flapping its wings in South America creates a typhoon in Japan. In the same way, our thoughts, feelings, beliefs and physical movements all have energy consequences and results.

A more immediate way to think about this is to imagine standing in a swimming pool. As you move, the water is displaced around your body although it is continually against your skin. You can see the ripple effect of the water's displacement. If you wave your hand in the air, the air is displaced. You can feel it even though you can't see it.

Your thoughts, feelings and desires also displace energy—the atoms and subatomic particles around you. You become aware of this by noticing, observing, feeling and appreciating (all words describing a receptive state). In this way, you receive what life is communicating and how it is responding to you. You have entered into a two-way relationship.

If most of your resources are invested in chasing after something, you lose awareness of your internal world and of how life is speaking to you. Yet, the river of life requires that you both paddle and ride the currents. Becoming adept at both helps you chart your course successfully.

When you write down your goal, you form a relationship with it. You have 50 percent; it has 50 percent. Throughout the ensuing weeks, your goal speaks to you through people, inner guidance, events and insights. It lets you know what would make you a better or more appropriate partner.

Your goal may change more than once as you become clearer about what you want. Some of what you receive may be difficult to hear; some will inspire you; some may surprise you.

In this multifaceted, dynamic relationship with your goal, it is important to stay current, as you would in any relationship, allowing yourself to be led by feedback and guidance. Practicing receiving helps you stay attentive to what your goal wants from you. Each time you rewrite your goal to integrate your current knowledge, life rearranges itself around you. A strong Receiver keeps the dialogue moving. And, with each new conversation, life rearranges itself yet again.

Take a moment to reread the introduction to this book. You have come a long way in your understanding of receiving! You know by now receiving is relaxing and energizing because you are no longer doing all of the work. Nor are you passive, waiting for the universe to do it all. Instead, you are part of a team with receiving and giving in balance.

The next section outlines everything you have learned about receiving. I've included tips and reminders to help you make the most of your Receive Practice.

practicing receiving

When I created the two-hours-a-week, five-week Receive and Manifest course, my premise was if we knew how to receive, life's inherent "givingness" would rush in as if a floodgate had been lowered. The results have been astounding. In the years that I have been teaching this process, it is clear to me that for this work to be successful, the following are essential:

- In the beginning, the order in which you learn and practice the exercises is important. I spent several years tweaking this course to strengthen its effectiveness, and I have found that the order matters. Once you are a skilled Receiver, it won't matter at all.
- Engage fully in each exercise. The more you immerse yourself in each exercise, the more you will receive from it.
- Do not rush this process. You've waited this long, so take your time. Attempting to *do more* is antithetical. Nobody becomes a skilled Receiver by *doing*. Like strengthening any muscle, when done too quickly, success is limited.
- Be consistent. If you don't do the exercises each day, they won't work. Strengthening your Receive Muscles requires day-to-day attentiveness to the givingness of life, a realistic appraisal of your present capabilities, and an understanding of how to utilize, maximize and interpret the

dynamic process, experiences and events that unfold.

The exercises in the following summary have been discussed in depth previously in this book. Refer to them to make sure you are getting the most out of each exercise.

For further inspiration, go to www.ThePowerofReceiving .com. There, you will find services, articles and products that support your Receive Practice.

a summary of the receive exercises

1. Take the Three Steps.
2. Commit to the Complaint Fast.
3. Review the Receptive States word list.
4. Write down your goal in one sentence.
5. Breathe in . . . and out . . .
6. Breathe in something you like about yourself . . . and out . . .
7. Breathe in something you don't like about yourself . . . and out . . .

8. Rewrite your goal if necessary.

9. Create a Monster Celebration.

10. Immerse yourself in a sixty-second experience of one of your five senses.

11. Write down your goal in the present tense as one of your five gratitudes.

12. Assess your relationship with your goal.

1. TAKE THE THREE STEPS

Step One: *Accept all compliments.*

The first step demonstrates to the universe, people and to your goal that you are ready to receive.

- Receive compliments, gifts, smiles—anything that is given to you.
- Accept them all gratefully and graciously.
- Once you receive the "little" things, you will easily graduate to the bigger ones.
- You are exercising your Receive Muscles so that you can receive your goal.

Step Two: *Count your blessings.*

Writing your five gratitudes each day strengthens receptivity and makes you attractive to your goal.

- Each day, write down five things for which you are grateful.
- Remember: What you focus on grows.
- If you focus on gratitude, you have more to be grateful for.
- Gratitude is a receptive state.
- The more time you spend in gratitude, the better Receiver you become.
- Choose one of your five gratitudes and spend sixty seconds visualizing yourself in that experience.

Step Three: *Be spiritually naked.*

Be self-revealing. Sharing all of who you are allows your goal to get to know the authentic you. Your goal can be more helpful when fully informed.

- Be self-revealing. Don't just trot out the healed or "together" parts of your personality.

- Look for opportunities to share what is going on with you.
- Be authentic; be real.
- When you include all of the parts of yourself, you will create a life in which others will do the same.
- Your goal loves a whole person. It is better informed about how to connect with you, dialogue with you and get close to you. You are giving your goal more data to work with.

2. COMMIT TO THE COMPLAINT FAST:
NO SUFFERING ALLOWED! NO SUFFERING ALOUD!
Complaints chase away your goal, just like they chase away people.

- Put your *No Suffering Allowed! No Suffering Aloud!* sign where you can see it each day. Put it on the refrigerator or take it to work. You can copy the one on page 78 in this book or get a free one from www.ThePowerofReceiving.com.
- A Complaint Fast allows the conditions you don't like to change.
- Not only does complaining scare away your goal

but complaining is about a story, not about your feelings.

- Suffering is about the past rather than the present, where all manifestation occurs.

3. REVIEW THE RECEPTIVE STATES WORD LIST

Your goal needs someone to receive it. You want this someone to be you! Every time you place yourself in a receptive state, your goal reaches you more easily.

- Review the Receptive States word list (in chapter 1) several times during the week.
- Throughout the day, pause to reflect, observe, listen, notice, etc. (all words from the Receptive States word list).
- Say *thank you* when you see a beautiful tree, gain an insight, observe a kindness.
- Notice if it is easy or difficult to enter a receptive state.

4. WRITE DOWN YOUR GOAL IN ONE SENTENCE

You are now ready to begin a relationship with your goal.

- Write your goal in one clear, specific sentence.
- Don't be anxious about grammar. You simply want to start the conversation with your goal.
- All you want now is to get on your goal's radar screen.
- This relationship will develop over time.

5. BREATHE IN . . . AND OUT . . .

This exercise helps you stay in the present, rather than the suffering past or the fantasy future. Every time you redirect your mind to the present, you are helping your goal connect with you.

- Bring your attention to your breath.
- As you breathe in, say to yourself silently: *Breathing in, I know I am breathing in.*
- As you breathe out, say to yourself silently: *Breathing out, I know I am breathing out.*
- Repeat this ten times. If you are pressed for time, repeat it five times.
- But don't wait until you have a leisurely afternoon to do it.

6. BREATHE IN SOMETHING YOU LIKE ABOUT YOURSELF . . . AND OUT . . .

* Think of something you like about yourself.
* Bring your attention to your breath.
* As you breathe in, say to yourself silently: *Breathing in, I'm breathing in [put in your own word or phrase], something I like about myself...*
* As you breathe out, say to yourself silently: *Breathing out, I'm breathing out [put in your own word or phrase], something I like about myself...*
* If you have time, repeat this ten times.
* If you are pressed for time, repeat it five times.

7. BREATHE IN SOMETHING YOU DON'T LIKE ABOUT YOURSELF . . . AND OUT . . .

* Think of something you don't like about yourself.
* Bring your attention to your breath.
* As you breathe in, say to yourself silently: *Breathing in, I'm breathing in [put in your own*

word or phrase], something I don't like about myself . . .

- As you breathe out, say to yourself silently: *Breathing out, I'm breathing out [put in your own word or phrase], something I don't like about myself . . .*
- If you have time, repeat this ten times.
- If you are pressed for time, repeat it five times.

While breathing in . . . and out . . . what you like and don't like about yourself

- You'll notice that you can relate to all feelings at one time or another.
- All of the things you like and don't like want to be in the Big Circle.
- Feelings are universal. There isn't a feeling that you've had, no matter how small, that isn't available to everyone else.
- It is it an important acknowledgment of your humanity to embrace all of your human experiences and feelings.
- This exercise is about inclusion and acceptance.
- This exercise encourages self-revelation. It takes the sting out of being human.

- This exercise helps to move you out of the strict "good person" role.
- This exercise encourages whatever is in the Little Circle to come into the Big Circle.

8. REWRITE YOUR GOAL IF NECESSARY

All relationships change over time. Keep current with new information, insights and changes that occur.

- You and your goal are in a conversation.
- Rewrite your goal if you both have decided on changes, improvements or even something else altogether.

9. CREATE A MONSTER CELEBRATION

Instead of embracing all of who we are, we tuck away certain parts. But they don't go anywhere. These run your life from behind the scenes (the Little Circle). They produce anxiety and interfere with your goal. They are the gatekeepers and stand between you and your goal. Just as you would help a shy person at a party to feel more comfortable, receive and embrace these outcasts. Help them feel accepted

and included. They have something to say to you. Listen to
them.

- Set up the room for a party. Since you are creating this party with your imagination, the sky's
  the limit! Spare no expense. Have fun with it.
- Once the room is set up, you are ready to receive
  your monster. When you first do this exercise,
  bring only one monster out.
- When the monster comes into the room, welcome
  it! You are the receiving line. Let it know that you
  are delighted to have it come to the party!
- Then, observe, dialogue and just see what
  happens. Stay with this part as long as feels
  comfortable.
- When the party is over, or when you feel the
  monster is ready to go back into the closet, you
  can begin to bring this exercise to an end.
- But before the monster goes back into the closet,
  it may want to tell you something or ask you
  something, or it may want something from you.
  Ask, if you feel comfortable doing so.
- Once the monster is back in the closet, come
  back to the present.

- Write in your journal about your monster, the events that occurred and impressions or insights you received.

10. IMMERSE YOURSELF IN A SIXTY-SECOND EXPERIENCE OF EACH OF YOUR FIVE SENSES

Each time you spend time tuning in to one of the senses, you are in a receptive state, which strengthens your Receive Muscles. This is also a surprisingly relaxing exercise.

- Throughout the day, bring your awareness to each of your five senses.
- For each one, spend sixty seconds immersed in that sense experience.
- You can do this anywhere—while you are walking your dog, sitting at a traffic light or when you are on hold during a phone call.

11. WRITE YOUR GOAL IN THE PRESENT TENSE AS ONE OF YOUR FIVE GRATITUDES

Now that you are well versed and experienced in receiving, this exercise helps you break the "time frame" habit when you focus on gratitude. Prior to this, however, Little Circle mavericks have too much power to make this an effective exercise.

- When you express gratitude, your brain does not make a distinction between the past and future.
- The experience of gratitude is in the present where all manifestation occurs.

12. ASSESS YOUR RELATIONSHIP WITH YOUR GOAL

Be attentive to what your goal is communicating to you.

- How are you two doing? Cozy? On the same page? In need of a couples' counselor?
- Are any Little Circle inhabitants weighing in?
- How is life rearranging around you?

As you answer these questions, you may want to write in your journal about everything you are receiving. That information will help you decide how to take the next step.

Turn the page to learn about additional resources for your Receive Practice.

acknowledgments

Although writing is a solo endeavor, so much of what is involved in creating a book is due to the hard work and generosity of others. I first want to thank everybody who has inspired, helped and supported me during the several years it has taken me to write *The Power of Receiving*.

I could never have received the knowledge I write about in this book or deepened my understanding of receiving without the people who participated in my Receive and Manifest courses and workshops. Their belief in me and the process, and their willingness to trust I was onto something, have touched me profoundly.

I have a special place in my heart for those who signed up for my first courses when I was still working out the kinks and who encouraged me to finish this book, believing I had an important contribution to make. In particular, I am grateful to Jane Landis McCarthy, who opened her home for many of the Receive groups. Thank you, Dawn Budetto, Vicki Mottershead, Darlene Elkins, Mary Ann Bohem, Judith Goldberg, Sondra Novo, Joe Campanella, Joan Schochor, Holly Riddel, Kathy Herrmann, Robyn Moore-Johnson, Susan Mack, Carol Ryba, Carol Dolan, Val Bishop, Margaret Mahoney, Demetrius Bagley, Beth Jarrett, Carmel DiPaolo, Karen Ward, Elaine Schiripo, Kris Estes, Gini Roberts, Gail Wingate, LaChelle Nelson and Mary Bleile. I feel honored to have met such amazing people.

Special thanks to Carol Burdette for teaching me the sixty-second sense exercise and for joining me during a writing hiatus for an unforgettable road trip.

I owe a special debt of gratitude to Dr. Christiane Northrup for her interest, encouragement and assistance. She has been my angel. Additionally, special thanks to another angel, Ronnie Gale Dreyer, whose help and support I will never underestimate or forget.

Thanks also to the following people who encouraged and supported me, whether by reading my manuscript, offering suggestions or listening to me when I needed to talk: Tricia Secretan, Nancy Dreyfus, Elizabeth Rose Campbell, Patricia Gagic, Mary DiGiulian, Kelli Harman, Toni Thomas, Jerry Dore, Rick Levine, Deborah Rivers, Yvonne Serensky, Linda Caplan and Ann Karen Dowd.

I could not have brought my book out into the world without the support and expertise of Bob Silverstein of Quicksilver Books, who is not only a fantastic agent but also a great guy. Thank you, Bob! Thanks to my editor at Tarcher/Penguin, Michael Solana, for his encouragement and for giving me the gift of his keen editorial eye. And finally, thank you, Joel Fotinos, for seeing my passion, "getting" my message and taking a chance on me. Every writer should be lucky enough to have such a wonderful and responsive publisher.

Albert Schweitzer said it so eloquently:

Sometimes our light goes out but is blown into flame by an encounter with another human being. Each of us owes the deepest thanks to those who have rekindled this inner light.

Thank you, everybody.

—Amanda

resources for additional support and inspiration

Books

Abram, David. *The Spell of the Sensuous: Perception and Language in a More-Than-Human World.* New York: Vintage Books, 1997.

Azim, Jamal, and Harvey McKinnon. *The Power of Giving: How Giving Back Enriches Us All.* New York: Jeremy P. Tarcher/Penguin, 2009.

Ban Breathnach, Sarah. *Simple Abundance: A Daybook of Comfort of Joy.* New York: Grand Central, 2009 (repr. ed.).

Beattie, Melody. *The New Codependency: Help and Guidance for Today's Generation.* New York: Simon & Schuster Paperbacks, 2009.

Chopra, Deepak. *The Seven Spiritual Laws of Success: A Practical Guide to the Fulfillment of Your Dreams.* San Raphael, CA: Amber-Allen, 1994.

Emoto, Masaru, and David A. Thayne. *The Hidden Messages in Water.* New York: Atria Books, 2005.

Hay, Louise. *Gratitude: A Way of Life.* Carlsbad, CA: Hay House, 1996.

Hendrix, Harville, and Helen Hunt. *Receiving Love: Transform Your Relationship by Letting Yourself Be Loved.* New York: Atria Books, 2005.

Hicks, Jerry and Esther. *Ask and It Is Given: Learning to Manifest Your Desires.* Carlsbad, CA: Hay House, 2004.

———. *The Law of Attraction: The Basics of the Teachings of Abraham.* Carlsbad, CA: Hay House, 2006.

McTaggart, Lynn. *The Field: The Quest for the Secret Force of the Universe.* New York: Harper Paperbacks, 2003.

Nhat Hanh, Thich. *The Miracle of Mindfulness.* Boston, MA: Beacon Press, 1999.

Ponder, Catherine. *The Dynamic Laws of Prosperity.* Englewood Cliffs, NJ: Prentice-Hall, 1962.

Journals

Owen, Amanda. *Count Your Blessings 365 Days a Year.*

————. *The Power of Receiving Journal.*

Products

• A variety of products that will help you with your Receive Practice can be found at www.ThePowerofReceiving.com.

Website

www.ThePowerofReceiving.com